When Your Soul Speaks...

...Listen

Kirsten D. Westbrook

Maát Neftali

ISBN #978-0-9908327-5-1

Printed in the United States of America

Cover designed by: Elizabeth York-Westbrook

Acknowledgements

For years, I have contemplated on what to write about, because I knew there was a book in me. This book started out as a dissertation for my Master's Degree in Psycho-Energetic Counseling from the Southwest University of Sacred Studies. It started out as a case study on three different women. My first iteration was an attempt to find truth in others and I told their story with such specificity that I lost myself. I was then told to rewrite it, only bearing my soul. It was one of the hardest things I've ever had to do. I had to dig deep into my own pain and find connection with my inner self. This book is about that connection and is filled with specific truths about my life starting from birth. When reading it in this way, the words will activate your soul rather than your curiosity around specific events in my life.

I'm eternally grateful to my younger, but wiser sister, who encouraged and advised me. She also proofread, designed the cover and edited this work. To my older sister and brother, I am grateful for their support and believing in me. I am grateful to my mother, who raised me to be the best version of myself and taught me what greatness looks like.

I want to thank my line sisters for always being there for me and never giving up on me. I also want to thank The Center for Bio-Vibrotational Science and fellow Scientists for helping me grow and evolve. Lastly, I want to thank you for attaining this book which is a process of activating the souls of women all around the world.

Table of Contents

Foreword

Dr. Robert York-Westbrook

A message to my sisters reading this book. While reading this book I want you to tap into the following areas of your self-psychology.

Self-Focus
There is a level of intricate detail, emotions and connection to your own physical reactions. Read this book from a comprehensive perspective allowing its wisdom to cover large quantities of self-dialogue without losing its flow.

Thoughtful
Revisit every stage presented and use these stages to attain mastery of your emotions and feelings.

Heartfelt
This book will cause you to remember and spill your emotions through the annals of a challenging self-history. Do not be afraid to be honest with yourself.

Heart-wrenching
Your life may have been filled with betrayal, physical and psychological abuse, disappointments and unexplained trauma. In each stage of your life you have had repeated male absence, domination, manipulation, and disappointment. You have not yet had a true encounter that would seem mutually satisfying. You have received one surprise after another with disappointments in which the general message has been abuse, being used, followed by rejection. This book is written to give you liberation from that; remember your soul has not been soiled.

Truthful
Be honest about what has happened, honest about how you felt, and see the moments where you could have escaped some of the difficulties, but timing simply did not marry wisdom.

Incomplete
Your story is not over and will not be until you come into your full purpose, overcome the things that you have been through and find the passion to help others do the same.

Preface

The following letter was written July 23, 2012 after I had a breakthrough of my purpose. This was when I realized that I had a story to tell and that my pain could help others. I knew I had to write about it and talk about it. I don't know if Oprah Winfrey ever saw this letter, but it was cleansing to write it. This was my beginning:

Dear Oprah,

I hope this message finds you in good spirits and in good health. I hope you can find the time to read this because I have a lot to say. Last night, I watched your two-show finale (The Oprah Surprise) on YouTube and then I watched your last show. I didn't catch it when it originally aired. I don't know why, but it was meant for me to watch it now. It was profound, and it did something to me.

I'm a school teacher at KIPP: Intrepid in Houston, TX, and we teach character values, and we have something called, "The Elite 8." At Kipp, we have an extended year where we teach the values. I'm a math teacher, but I did not teach math these past two and a half weeks. I taught on these 8 values, which are: Social Intelligence, Self-Control, Love, Humor, Zest, Gratitude, Grit and Hope. I saw all these values in your show, and I kept thinking, "I need to show this to my kids." I saw so much love and gratitude, and I've been telling my students, "It doesn't matter how smart you are or how many degrees you have. If you do not have these character values, no one will hire you or want to work for you." I tell them, "It's

nice to be important, but it's more important to be nice." I cried and cried and could feel the love as they kept surprising you. Then I saw one of our schools: KIPP: Believe, featured on your show. And I knew that I really needed to show this now. I saw how much you valued education and how it was a teacher that changed your life. I think I cried the hardest when the Morehouse men graced the stage. I used your story as an example when I taught "Grit" and learned something about you that I did not know. It was that you had a child when you were 14 and lost that baby. I've gone through that. My son died three years ago. What I've been through in life can be summed up in the movie, "For Colored Girls." I could relate to almost every character- from rape, molestation, losing a child- to the words of family members disempowering you. I know that words can break a person's spirit, but they can also set you free.

I wanted you to know that, your words have set me free. After watching the 2-day surprise, then I watched your final show. Something woke up inside of me. I have been listening to Les Brown, Tony Robbins, Jim Rohn and I've read: Think and Grow Rich, The Magic of Believing, The Magic of Thinking Big, etc. And because my thinking is changing, I was able to receive your message. You said, "When your life is speaking to you, listen." I want to change lives one word at a time. My life is telling me that the classroom is not enough; you are not reaching enough people. I have a greatness inside of me that is burning to come out. I majored in the wrong thing in college-thinking about what could get me a "good job" versus finding out who I really am. When I would recite my poetry in front of people, it felt good. When I gave speeches, it felt right. But my

major was Finance. That was not who I was or who I am. I affected people- my words helped them. I don't know why I did not pursue my dreams and goals. Maybe it was fear of success instead of fear of failure. It is time for me to get out of my own way and start listening to my soul. I wanted you to know that your words have started to set me free. My life and my soul started speaking to me and I just kept crying and crying. I call them "Freedom Tears" because I don't think people really realize what freedom is. I know that one day I will be a world-renowned motivational speaker, and I will change lives one word at a time, whether it be written or oratory. I really do appreciate you and I really hope you find these words and know that you really have affected me. The feeling that I feel inside myself right now - The best way I can explain it is like when you are sitting in church and the pastor says something and you feel like he is speaking to you directly. You feel something in your chest and you just start to cry. You want to jump up out your seat and shout. That's what your words have done to me.

I have been reading those books and listening to those speakers because I've been trying to figure out who I am and where I'm supposed to be. Because I know that this is not it. I used to think that freedom of the mind is knowing where you come from, but I was wrong. Freedom is knowing where you are going. I am more than a teacher. I am more than a mother. I am more than a wife. I am more than a daughter. I am more than a sister. I am more. I am more.

Thank you,
Kirsten Westbrook

Part I: Introduction

The soul is the spiritual part of humans regarded in its moral aspect. The answers we seek are always there, but without a connection to your soul or universal consciousness, you block your ability to hear what the soul has to say. Therefore, you cannot live in your purpose. Psycho-energetic counseling is a revered therapeutic technique based on a vigorous connection between the psycho emotional links of social involvement and the energetic links of our existences. Through this type of counseling, a person can begin to heal, discover their purpose and live it. Emotional trauma dormant within our subconscious can block our natural energy flow called chakras, therefore hindering us from discovering our purpose. If these traumas are not dealt with, a person can fall victim to other experiences that they pull into their energy field causing them to spiral into a deep depression. This low vibrating state affects every aspect of your life because it affects your decision-making and causes you to misread situations and experiences. Psycho-energetics is important to the entire human species, especially those that are struggling to discover and live their true-life purpose. There are three main types of human beings and each type is affected by emotional trauma in a different way. The first type is the Sentient Being, the second type is the Conscious Being and the third type is the Ascended Master.

My method will focus on helping individuals listen intuitively to the Psychologists within themselves for the answers they seek; to listen to their souls. Facing past traumas to discover your energy type and emotional type will help examine every part of you so you can learn how to listen and

live in your purpose. I will analyze my own life to discover which type of Being I am by examining how I have dealt with my own personal past traumas. I will show that my method of looking deep within and getting the answers from yourself, has helped me discover who I am, how I improved my life and how I survived. Knowing your energy type and emotional type can help each type of Being start the steps to healing.

Energy types are connected to the four elements, and they are air, water, fire, and earth. This can be discovered using your year of birth. In the Center for Bio-Vibrational Science, we refer to this method in the Bio-Vibrational Wellness Program as *The Bio-Vibrational Wheel of Element Identification (BWEI)*. However, emotional types are more connected to your personal experiences and emotional traumas and how you have dealt with them.

I will give real examples of traumatic experiences and how the techniques mentioned have affected me. I will discuss ways to determine human intention and chakra healing with a ritual I have created to show how traumas can block certain chakras that can be opened with psycho-energetic counseling and spiritual technologies. Furthermore, I will discuss emotional energy, how to discover your life's purpose; how the breath relates to our healing; how diet affects our energy and emotions and why people fail.

Can spirituality be used to heal someone's psychology? Psychologists and Psychiatrists may argue that one has nothing to do with the other. In their studies, mental illness and depression is a physical issue. Psycho-energetic counseling deals with the soul and spirit. In the past decades, spirituality and energy healing has become more and more acceptable. There are those who deem themselves as spiritual life coaches and spiritual

healers through chakra cleansing, equine healing, qigong and reiki (to name a few). All these different methods can be researched and tried.

Definition of key terms:

The following terms are key terms that are useful to help understand the language of Psycho-energetic counselors and spiritual therapy.

Spiritual Therapy: serves the purpose of restoring your mental, emotional, physical and spiritual health (i.e. stone-work, aromatherapy, reiki healing, chanting mantras, burning incense).

Emotions: An affective state of consciousness in which joy, sorrow, fear, hate or the like, is experienced, as distinguished from cognitive and volitional tastes of consciousness.

Sentient Being: Those who are capable of experiencing suffering and who operate using the five senses: see, touch, smell, hear and taste; approval addicts that live life based on fate.

Conscious Being: A being connected to universal consciousness and lives beyond the five senses; lives purpose based on destiny.

Ascended Master: One who embodies the discipline necessary to do the work of the Neteru (Gods, Masters, Universe); has been on this terrestrial plane before and chose to come back for the sake of humanity.

Intention: An act or instance of determining mentally upon some action or result.

Energy Type: Energy associated with the four elements: air, water, fire and earth.

Emotional Type: This is the filter through which you see the world, the default setting of your personality to which you

revert, especially during stress. It represents your basic tendencies.

My ideas are supported by: <u>The Quantum Theory of Self-Empowerment</u> written by Dr. Robert York-Westbrook, <u>Q2</u> by Dr. Robert York-Westbrook; <u>Positive Energy</u> by Judith Orloff, <u>You Can Heal Your Life</u> by Louise Hay; <u>The Flight of the Narcissist</u> by Dr. Robert York-Westbrook, and <u>The Book of Chakra Healing</u> by Liz Simpson.

Chapter 1

Chakra System

With each trauma, we will analyze which parts of our energy system that were blocked in order to determine the best Psycho-energetic counseling needed. This energy system is made up of seven main chakras.

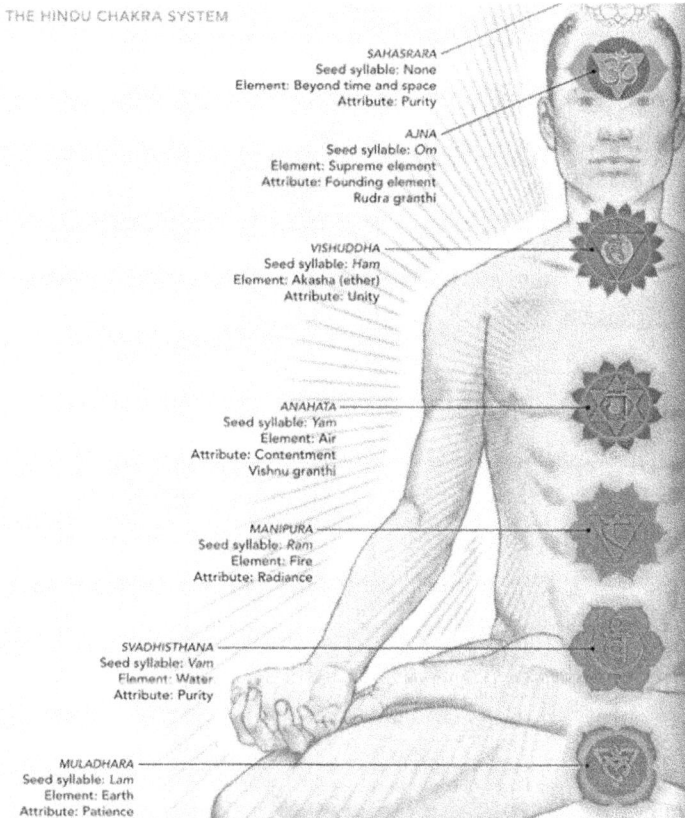

THE HINDU CHAKRA SYSTEM

SAHASRARA
Seed syllable: None
Element: Beyond time and space
Attribute: Purity

AJNA
Seed syllable: Om
Element: Supreme element
Attribute: Founding element
Rudra granthi

VISHUDDHA
Seed syllable: Ham
Element: Akasha (ether)
Attribute: Unity

ANAHATA
Seed syllable: Yam
Element: Air
Attribute: Contentment
Vishnu granthi

MANIPURA
Seed syllable: Ram
Element: Fire
Attribute: Radiance

SVADHISTHANA
Seed syllable: Vam
Element: Water
Attribute: Purity

MULADHARA
Seed syllable: Lam
Element: Earth
Attribute: Patience

Figure 1: The Chakra System

Each chakra is related to a definite part of the body or organ which it provides with the energy it requires to function. Every chakra corresponds to a precise feature of human behavior and development. Our circular spirals of energy vibrate at diverse stages in relation to the awareness of the individual and their capacity to assimilate the characteristics of each into their life. The lower chakras are connected with essential emotions and needs, for the energy here vibrates at a lower frequency and is therefore denser in nature. The advanced energies of the upper chakras parallel to our higher mental and spiritual ambitions and abilities.

How open or how easily the energies flow through our chakras determines our state of well-being and stability. Awareness of our more delicate energy system empowers us to maintain balance and harmony on the physical, mental and spiritual level. All meditation and yoga methods seek to balance out the energy of the chakras by cleansing the lower energies and guiding them upwards. Life events, traumas and how we deal with them play a crucial part in the flow of our energy system. Once closed, there are many ways to tap into each chakra to open it back up. Although it is possible to have some open chakras and some closed chakras, all chakras need to be clear for the entire system to flow and to be in tune with universal consciousness. Grounding and living consciously with an awareness of how we attain and devote our energy, we become capable of balancing our life force with our mental, physical and spiritual selves.

To become fully self-realized and in harmony with our physical and spiritual nature our denser lower energies need to be harmonized with the lighter energies of the upper centers. This is to say our survival and base tendencies must be raised to

incorporate a heart-felt spiritual focus expressed in all areas of our Being. Indeed, each of the upper-level energies corresponds and refines a lower level counterpart: 7th with 1st, 6th with 2nd, 5th with 3rd. In the center of our being is full integration into the heart.

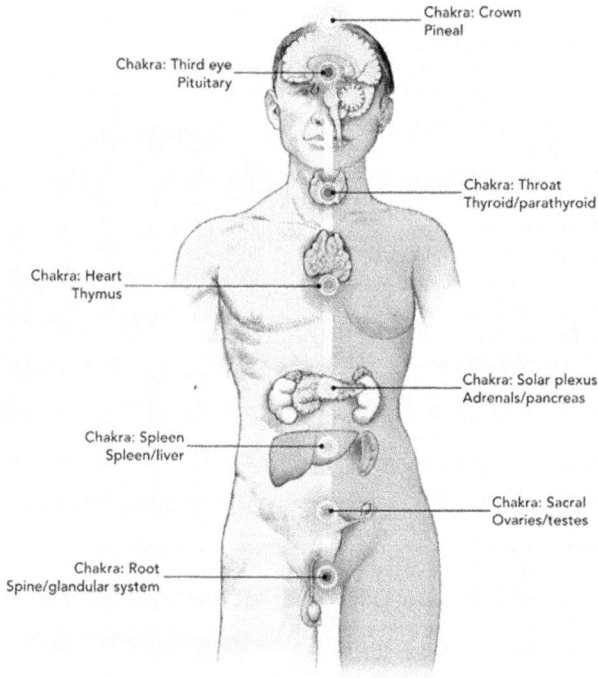

CHAKRAS AND THE ENDOCRINE SYSTEM

Chakra: Crown
Pineal

Chakra: Third eye
Pituitary

Chakra: Throat
Thyroid/parathyroid

Chakra: Heart
Thymus

Chakra: Solar plexus
Adrenals/pancreas

Chakra: Spleen
Spleen/liver

Chakra: Sacral
Ovaries/testes

Chakra: Root
Spine/glandular system

Figure 2: Chakra System and Endocrine System

Chakras and the Endocrine System

The chakra system is our energy system, but it is also physical. The 7 main chakras correspond directly with the endocrine system - which is the master command center of the human body for the production and regulation of our hormones. The endocrine system is the collection of glands that produce hormones that regulate metabolism, growth and development, tissue function, sexual function, reproduction, sleep, and mood, among other things. The endocrine system is made up of the pituitary gland, thyroid gland, parathyroid glands, adrenal glands, pancreas, ovaries (in females) and testicles (in males).

The endocrine system encompasses several glands that produce the hormones, acting as chemical messengers, that are secreted into the bloodstream from specific organs to arouse or impede physical processes. By adjusting the hormone levels, the endocrine system works to preserve the body in a state of ideal health. The chakras are linked with the glands responsible for creating the hormones. As shown in Figure 2, the positions of the chakras correspond to the locations of the glands in the endocrine system and influence their functioning. When energy is blocked in one of the chakras, the running of the corresponding gland may be transformed, therefore creating imbalance in the construction of hormones. By dissipating the blocked energy from the chakra, balance will be reestablished, and the hormones production regulated.

The following is a detailed breakdown of each chakra, how they relate to the Endocrine System and how they work. To help clear your blocked charkas, I will discuss how to set up an altar and some exercises you can do to get the energy flowing. There are certain crystals that can be worn on the body or placed on the altar to aid in unlocking your energy system. This along with the proper meditation can truly turn your life around.

Root Chakra (Muladhara meaning root or support)

The first chakra is the Root Chakra, located at the base of the spine; it is red in color. The Root Chakra focuses on birth

issues, survival patterns, generational patterns, money, food and health issues. "This chakra is closely linked to our primal instinct, incorporating our fundamental needs for shelter, food, and security in short our survival instinct." (York-Westbrook, 2010, p. 101) When your Root Chakra is closed, you struggle with weight and body issues; you frequently struggle with debt and lack of money; and you carry an underlying sense of not being worth it and not belonging. When your Root Chakra is balanced, you are content with your body. You are confident with money, managing it, and will always have enough for what you need and want. You also feel like you belong and have a strong connection with your family and/or friends. As a result, you feel wanted and loved. If too open, you tend to be a bully, overly materialistic, and self-centered. The adrenals are the glands that correlates to the Root Chakra.

The adrenals are triangular-shaped glands that cap each of the kidneys. They secrete a variety of hormones including those that regulate the body's metabolism of fats, proteins, and carbohydrates and ones that control the balance of salt in our bodily fluids. These glands also produce adrenalin, the hormone essential for our primitive "flight or fight" response, from which we can determine the link between this gland and the Root Chakras' association with the issue of physical survival (Simpson, 2013, p. 14-15).

The Seven Chakras							
Chakra #	1st Chakra	2nd Chakra	3rd Chakra	4th Chakra	5th Chakra	6th Chakra	7th Chakra
Chakra Name	Root Chakra	Sacral Chakra	Solar Chakra	Heart Chakra	Throat Chakra	Third Eye Chakra	Crown Chakra
Sanskrit Name	Muldhara Chakra	Svadhishthana Chakra	Manipura Chakra	Anahata Chakra	Vishuddha Chakra	Ajna Chakra	Sahasrara Chakra
Location	Base of Spine	Below the Navel	Below the Chest	Center of Chest	Throat	Center of Forehead Above Eyebrows	Top of Head
Color	Red	Orange	Yellow	Green	Blue	Indigo	Violet
Musical Note	C	D	E	F	G	A	B
Balanced Attributes	Stability	Sexuality	Self-Esteem	Self-Love	Communication	Intuition	Divine Connection
Imbalanced Attributes	Scattered Energies	Sexual Dysfunction	Low Self Esteem	Depression	Shy Withdrawn	Lack of Direction	Cynicism
Location of Physical Issues	Legs Feet	Reproductive Organs	Intestines Stomach	Heart Circulatory System	Throat Lungs Sinuses Thyroid	Eyes Ears	Brain
Crystal Therapy	Obsidian Jet Hematite	Garnet Ruby	Tigers Eye Yellow Calcite	Malachite Rose Quartz	Sodalite	Azurite Lapis Lazuli	Amethyst Ametrine
Essential Oil Therapy	Patchouli Oil	Ylang Ylang Oil	Neroli Oil	Chamomile Oil	Peppermint Oil	Sandalwood Oil	Frankincense Oil
Nature Therapy	Gardening Hiking and Earth Sitting	Sexual Expression and Creative Expression	Sunshine Sunbathing and Practicing Healthy Boundaries	Self-Time and Pampering Yourself	Singing Chanting Toning and Meaningful Discussions	Dreaming of Possibilites Releasing Preconceived Notions	Meditation Looking to the Heavens Cloud Watching Star Gazing

Figure 3: The Seven Chakras and their Meanings
Sacral Chakra (Swadhisthana meaning sweetness)

The second chakra is the Sacral Chakra located right below the belly button. The objective of the Sacral Chakra is sexuality, the nature of your relationships, freedom from guilt, pleasure and nurturance, sensation and creativity. The color is orange. "In other words, this powerhouse of energy has the potential to provide you with the basis to form meaningful relationships with self, and others." (York-Westbrook, 2010, p. 102) When closed, you believe sex is bad and that it can hurt you. You are oversensitive; causing you to feel abused, hurt, and confused. You don't trust that you can be loved just for being you. However, if the Sacral Chakra is balanced, you enjoy

pleasure in many ways in life. You create healthy sexual experiences with others that honor you. You also have a strong sense of your sexuality and recognize it as one of your most powerful creative energies. A Sacral Chakra that is spinning too fast will cause emotional unbalance, making you manipulative and sexually addictive (Simpson, 2013, p. 50). The gland associated with the second chakra are the ovaries for a female or testes for a male.

> The male and female reproductive organs, or gonads, produce hormones that are responsible for the development of secondary sexual characteristics, such as the depth of voice and amount of body hair. The testes and ovaries control an individual's sexual development and maturity as well as the production of sperm in males and eggs in females. Our relationship with our own sexuality, and issues of emotional balance concerning that, is a key association of this chakra (Simpson, 2013, p. 15).

Solar Plexus Chakra (Manipura meaning lustrous gem)

The yellow chakra is the Solar Plexus Chakra, also referred to as your Personal Power Chakra. It is the center of your total physical well-being. (York-Westbrook, 2010, p. 135) This chakra deals with your relationship with yourself and your personal power. How you view yourself, level of self-esteem, freedom from shame, your self-worth and personal thoughts and image of self are all connected to this chakra. When the Solar Plexus Chakra is closed, you feel like a victim in the world and you often feel powerless to other people and circumstances. You tend to give your power away to others, which you feel is

necessary to keep peace in relationships. These feelings cause you to suffer from stomach pains and anxiety. However, when this chakra is open, you have a strong sense of your own power and how to use it in healthy ways and for good in the world. You have no problem admiring others with power and influence. In fact, you may choose to emulate those who use their power to make a difference in the world. However, if too open, you tend to be angry and controlling. You feel superior, therefore causing you to be judgmental. The Pancreas gland is related to this chakra.

> The pancreas lies behind the stomach and secretes a variety of substances essential for the effective digestion of food. It also produces insulin, which helps control the blood's sugar level. One of the physical dysfunctions of this chakra is diabetes, a disease accused by excess sugar in the blood stream. There is a further link with the solar Plexus and adrenaline, which is why we experience "butterflies in the stomach" during frightening experiences. The associated body part is the digestive system and a further dysfunction of this chakra are stomach ulcers (Simpson, 2013, p. 15).

Heart Chakra (Anahata meaning unstruck)

The Heart Chakra allows us to feel more appreciation and gratitude in life. Green in color, it is located in the center of the chest. This is your emotional zone, where you tap into your compassion, love, the feeling of touch, and devotion. If you are afraid of commitment and you feel like you have to please others to be loved, your Heart Chakra is probably closed. Being hurt by others over and over again in relationships will cause you to put

your guard up and stay closed off from others. Once this chakra is balanced, you feel very comfortable in your relationships and you give and receive love with ease. Having that feeling of gratitude makes it easy to forgive without feeling sorry for anyone. If the Heart Chakra is too open, you are possessive, loves conditionally, withholds emotionally to punish and you are overly dramatic. The Thymus is the gland that corresponds to the Heart chakra.

> Located just above the heart, for thymus produces hormones that stimulate general growth, particularly early in life. It also has a purifying role in the body stimulating the production of lymphocytes, which form part of the blood's white cells' defense system, attacking invading organisms and providing immunity. Scientists now recognize that auto-immune diseases, where the immune system attacks its own proteins, mistaking them for a foreign substance, have an emotional link and are not simply due to physical or environmental causes (Simpson, 2013, p. 15).

The Heart Chakra is the central chakra that is the passage through which we move from the lower to the higher centers, shifting us from the realm of basic needs into the realm of blessings.

Throat Chakra (Vishuddha meaning purification)

Speaking your truth and having a voice comes from the Throat Chakra, which is blue in color. It is located in the hollow of the throat. Not only using your voice and coming from the center of your will power, this chakra is also about listening and being heard. Communication is key. A blocked Throat Chakra

can be the result of a person being afraid to speak up and say what they want or how they feel. You hold back from self-expression and go along and agree with others due to the fear of upsetting them. On the other hand, if you are comfortable speaking your truth and knows what it feels like to hold an audience because you inspire people to listen, your Throat Chakra is open. You feel like you are heard and honored for your truth. If too open, you will tend to be loquacious, dogmatic, self-righteous and arrogant. This chakra corresponds to the Thyroid or Parathyroid gland.

> The thyroid gland, situated on either side of the larynx and trachea in the neck, manufactures thyroxine, which controls the bodies metabolic rate – that is, how effectively it converts food into energy. Behind this lies the parathyroid gland, which controls the level of calcium in the blood stream. In addition to physical growth, these glands are also believed to affect one's mental development. The Throat Chakra, linked with all forms of communication, corresponds to the need for balance between the rational, cerebral approach and emotional expression of the heart (Simpson, 2013, p. 13).

Third Eye Chakra (Ajna meaning to know)

The Third Eye Chakra or Intuitive Chakra is the 6th chakra, indigo in color and connected to the eyes, ears, sinuses and lower brain. It is located in the middle of the forehead. Here is where intuition and psychic talents reside. The ability for self-reflection, visualization, discernment and trusting yourself. If this chakra is blocked, you feel disconnected from your intuition, or don't feel like you have any. You feel lost when it

comes to your spiritual purpose and path in life; you fear success. You may get headaches and feel tension in your brow area often. When balanced, your intuition is your constant guide that you trust. You have a strong sense of your own inner truth and listen to and follow it as it guides you on your life path. You are not attached to material things and you act on confidence based on your intuition. When your Third Eye Chakra is too open, you are an authoritarian and arrogant. The pituitary gland is connected to this Chakra.

> The pituitary gland is located within a structure at the base of the skull. Once called "master gland" of the endocrine system, it has since been found to be controlled by hormonal substances released by the hypothalamus, a part of the brain. This vital gland influences growth, metabolism, and general body chemistry. This includes the hormone which produces contractions during labor and releases milk from the breasts during lactation. It is interesting to note this Third-Eye pituitary gland connection with birth and motherhood, a time when many women feel that their intuition, particularly with regard to their child, is at its peak (Simpson, 2013, p. 15-16).

Crown Chakra (Sahasrara meaning thousand-fold)

The seventh chakra is violet in color and is located at the top of the head, thus called the Crown Chakra. "The Crown Chakra further expands the concepts introduced by work on the Throat and Third Eye Chakras- communication and inter-connectedness with all things and all knowledge" (Simpson, 2013, p. 118). The energy of the Crown Chakra influences your

experience with charity, connection to the universe, belief systems and divine consciousness. When your Crown Chakra is closed, you feel no connection or guidance from a higher power. You may feel unworthy of help from the universe or spirit, which causes you to be angry and feel abandoned. When open, or balanced, you feel a strong connection with a higher power and are confident that you are protected and watched over. You know that you are deserving of blessings and are grateful. However, if this chakra is spinning too fast, you could be psychotic or a manic depressive. You may be confused, frustrated and have a sense of unrealized power. The Crown Chakra is connected to the Pineal Gland.

> The glandular connection of the Crown Chakra is the pineal gland, a pea-sized body that lies deep within the brain and was once thought to serve no useful purpose. Considered in the seventeenth century to be the seat of the soul by French philosopher, Rene' Descartes, resent scientific research has linked this gland with the production of melatonin and regulates our internal "body clock." Melatonin is also the subject of intense scientific interest for its possible anti-ageing properties and is believed to affect the pituitary, thyroid, adrenals, and gonads- although no one yet understands how or why. Like the Crown's function within the chakra system as a whole, the pineal gland is the control center for the effected functioning of our physical, emotional, and mental selves. (Simpson, 2013, p. 216)

I will use the Chakra System to help analyze my life experiences and how I was affected by them. This will determine how traumatic experiences can block certain chakras and how a

21

blocked energy system can hinder you from living your purpose and being able to listen to that inner voice. Closed chakras can affect your everyday life, while open chakras can empower you to make the right decisions and life just flows for you.

Chapter 2

Emotional and Energy Types

To pin down your style of how you relate emotionally, it's important to know your emotional type. This is the filter through which you see the world, the default setting of your personality to which you revert, especially during stress. It represents your basic tendencies. You can build on these by making the most of your best traits and adopting traits from the other types that appeal to you. Judith Orloff, M.D., is the innovator behind Energy Psychiatry. Through her psychiatric practice, she has observed four main Emotional Types. It is possible to identify with more than one, however, most of us will identify more with one than the others. Knowing your type can deliver awareness into how you interrelate with others and will help you master your emotions instead of merely responding when you get upset. Dealing with emotions effectually isn't stuffing them away or feeling them less. It's about inaugurating stability, strengthening those areas where you're most exposed and making the most of your assets. The following is a brief summary of each Emotional Type adapted from her book, Emotional Freedom: Liberate Yourself from Negative Emotions and Transform Your Life:

> **Type #1. The Intellectual: Intense Thinker**
> Intellectuals are bright, articulate, incisive analysts who are most comfortable in the mind. The world is powerfully filtered through rational thought. Known for keeping their cool in heated situations, they often struggle with emotions, don't trust their guts, are slow to engage in anything light-hearted, sensual, or playful.

Are you an intellectual?

Do you believe that you can think your way to any solution? When presented with a problem, do you immediately start analyzing the pros and cons rather than noticing how it makes you feel? Do you prefer planning to being spontaneous? Does your overactive mind prevent you from falling asleep?

If so, try this:

- Breathe. If you're mentally gridlocked simply inhale and exhale deeply, in through your nose out through your mouth.

- Exercise. Whether you're walking, rollerblading, or lifting weights, exercise creates an acute body awareness that relaxes a busy mind.

- Empathize. Ask yourself, "How can I respond from my heart, not just my head." Empathize before trying to fix a problem with loved ones too quickly.

Type #2. The Empath: Emotional Sponge
Empaths are highly sensitive, loving, and supportive. They are highly tuned instruments when it comes to emotions and tend to feel everything, sometimes to an extreme.

Are you an empath?

Have you been called "too emotional" or "overly sensitive"? If a friend is upset do you start feeling it too? Do you replenish your energy by being alone and tend to get exhausted in crowds? Are you sensitive to noise, smells, and excessive talking?

If so, try this:

- Take calming mini-breaks throughout the day. Go outside for a walk, meditate in your room alone. Focus on exhaling pent up emotions such as anxiety or fear so they don't lodge in your body.

- Protect your sensitivities. Make a list of your top five most emotionally rattling situations, then formulate a plan for handling them so you don't get caught in a panic. For instance, take your own car places so you don't get trapped in social situations. (For more strategies see my previous blog "Are You an Empath?")

Type #3. The Rock. Strong and Silent Type Consistent, dependable, and stable; they will always show up for you. You can express emotions freely around them— they won't get upset or judge. But they often have a hard time expressing their own feelings, and their mates are always trying to get them to express emotions.

Are you a rock?

Is it easier for you to listen than to share your feelings? Do you often feel like you are the most dependable person in the room? Are you generally satisfied with the status quo in relationships (though others try to draw you out emotionally)?

If so, try this:

- Stir things up. Begin to initiate emotional exchanges instead of simply responding to them. Remember that showing emotions is a form of passion and generosity too.

- Express a feeling a day. In a daily journal, write down an emotion you're experiencing. Don't hold back. Are you pissed off? Content? In love? Whatever you feel, bravo! Tell someone. Express the emotion.

Type #4. The Gusher. Attuned to emotions Gushers are in touch with their emotions and love to share them. No one has to wonder where they're at. Gushers are able to quickly process negativity and move on. Their downside is that they tend to share "too much information" and over-sharing can burn people out.

Are you a gusher?

Do you get anxious if you keep your feelings in? When a problem arises is your first impulse to pick up the phone and share? Do you have trouble sensing other people's emotional boundaries?

If so, try this:

- Before seeking support, tune into your intuition. Spend a few quiet moments going inward to find out what your gut says. Try to solve the situation from a calm centered place. See what flashes or "ah-has" come to you. Take time to build your own emotional muscles.

The most important relationship you'll ever have is with yourself. If this is good, you'll be able to have wonderful relationships with others. Knowing your emotional type provides a platform to emotionally evolve and to become a truly powerful person (Orloff, 2009, p. 101-109).

Energy Types

Carol Tuttle is a teacher, speaker, healer, and best-selling author of five books. She has dedicated her life to helping people worldwide create the lives and relationships they desire. She blogs to support you in creating your ideal life. Tuttle created Four Types which come from the four most common elements in living organisms: nitrogen, oxygen, hydrogen and carbon. Each of these elements is associated with Air, Water, Fire and Earth. They are also connected to a State of Matter: Gas, Liquid, Plasma and Solid. There are four types of energy movement in the world. You express one of them in your thoughts, feelings and behaviors. The Nitrogen type is bright and animated and upbeat. The Oxygen type is soft and calming and likes to make plans and gather details. The Hydrogen type is swift and dynamic, and the Carbon type is structured and exact.

In my research, I connected these energy types to The Cosmological Medicine wheel or Bio-vibrational Wheel of Elemental Identification (BWEI), which is a process using your full birth name and birth date to determine what element was dominate at the time of your birth and your spirit energy: Earth, Water, Nature, Fire and Mineral. Notice, this method has five Elements instead of four. Combined, these methods give a very detailed insight into a person's spiritual energy system. In helping understand and realizing my life purpose, I performed the Bio-Vibrational Wheel of Element Identification (BWEI) on my birth name. As an Ascended Master, I received my Spiritual name, Maát Hayyala Neftali in 2012. This name means, "Warrior for truth and justice who is the daughter of Ja." It takes a person five years to fully charge a new name and become one with it.

Type 1: Air- Nitrogen – Gas

The Nitrogen Type is directly correlated to the Element Air. These people are relaxed, bright, animated and they have a gift for new ideas and possibilities. Although, if these ideas are not being executed, it may mean this person does not follow through. The direction of this type is Upward, and the quality is Light.

Type 2: Water – Oxygen- Liquid

Type two are people that are soft and calming. Their gift is gathering details. They like to have a plan and gather information by asking questions. However, in the gathering of information, it may cause them to move too slow or be too detailed. This personality is flowing and elegant in nature. Their direction is Inward and their quality is Soft.

Type 3: Fire – Hydrogen- Plasma

Type three can be described as a swift and dynamic person who is comfortable with themselves. They have a gift for quickly moving into action to create practical and lasting results. They have a great work ethic and are focused on getting the job done. However, they may move too quickly and come across as pushy. The quality is active and reactive, while the direction is outward.

Type 4: Earth- Carbon- Solid

Type four is a structured and exact person who has the gift for looking at the world through critical eyes and perfecting it. They reflect keenly on the bigger picture and focus on what

can be done to make things better. Nonetheless, being a perfectionist may cause them to stall because things are not perfect enough. The quality is Rigid and Bold and their direction is Still.

Chapter 3

Bio-Vibrational Wheel of Elemental Identification

The Dagara Cosmological Medicine wheel was introduced to the West by Malidoma Somé. Malidoma Somé is an initiated Elder into the Dagara Tribe of West Central Africa. He is also the holder of a Ph.D. in Political Science from the Sorbonne, and a second Ph.D. in English Literature from Brandeis. He has written several books, including Of Water and the Spirit and The Healing Wisdom of Africa. He now travels the world providing workshops to share the traditional wisdom and spirit of Africa. The Cosmological Medicine Wheel or Bio-Vibrational Wheel of Elemental Identification (BWEI), is a spiritual instrument providing perception into our life purpose and the energy disparities that may be averting us from reaching our purpose. It is not used as a future telling tool or a "reading"; it is for guidance and insight. I use it to help interpret that inner voice when we receive guidance from within. There are no absolutes; meaning that matters of the spirit are fluid and always shifting. The Dagara tribe of West Central Africa efficaciously classify their people into five different categories: fire, water, mineral, earth and nature. These are shown below on the Dagara African Wheel with the colors the Dagara normally associate with each type. Each of the five types of people play a very precise role.

Every person born into this world comes from one of these categories in order to help accomplish the kind of purpose that that class of people is supposed to fulfill in order to contribute to the community to help maintain it.

The Cosmological Medicine Wheel or BWEI is the beginning of the self-reflection process. We all should exercise spiritual discipline when going through the self-reflection process so that we may better understand the context of our elemental makeup assigned to us at birth. The spirit world aligned our elements in a certain way serving as a spiritual survival kit. This was to assist us in dealing with our initial life experiences. For Example, you might have been born with limited fire energy. It was likely because too much fire would have destroyed you.

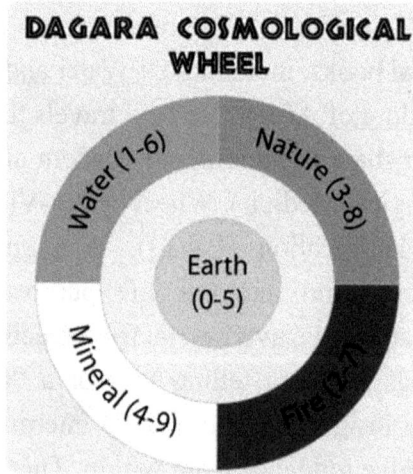

DAGARA COSMOLOGICAL WHEEL

Water (1-6)

Nature (3-8)

Earth (0-5)

Mineral (4-9)

Fire (2-7)

Figure 4: Dagara Wheel (Water-blue; Nature-green; Fire-red; Mineral-white; Earth-yellow)

The issue is that in most cases we weren't aware of any of the above, therefore, we never discovered our elemental makeup inhibiting us from finding our purpose thus, preventing us from evolving as our circumstances changed. For example, you may not have initially needed a lot of fire when you were born but over time your circumstances changed possibly requiring more. However, due to your lack of fire you're unable to ignite that element when needed.

The Cosmological Medicine Wheel or BWEI is the beginning of our journey; it is not intended to be a cure all to our problems nor does it crystallize our purpose. Discovering how to live in your purpose is something that you will discover using Psycho-energetic Counseling techniques.

Overview of the Elements

Dagara cosmology begins with the story of conception as a burning planet, a ball of fire combusted at high speed. Thus, Fire is the first element of the Dagara wheel. When this moving, burning sphere encountered Water, things changed. The shock of their meeting drove fire into the underworld, leaving the surface as a hot steamy place, fertile for breeding all kinds of life. This is Earth, the third element. The hard components of the earth, which provide structure and connection, are Mineral, the fourth element. Meanwhile steam formed atmosphere around the earth. As steam expanded, its pressure began to subside, giving birth to the fifth element, Nature. (http://www.englishwordplay.com/healingwisdom.html)

1. **Fire:** Fire is the original element; to which everything returns. It is the state the ancestors are in. Shamans fit into this category, because they live in two worlds. A fire person lives in the future and therefore finds the average person too slow. He or she can be seen as

impatient. If a person or culture forgets their connection with the other worlds, they may rush headlong into destruction. A fire culture can be a war culture. However, a fire person's fire may be translated into a warm, gentle flame that keeps a community aware of its relationship with other worlds.

2. **Water**. The elders say that it came from the Other World and spilled into the earth at the moment that the veil between the two worlds was thinned. We are all the children of water. Without the "water of life" nothing can be purified. It is essential to the spiritual journey. It bestows serenity. Pollution is the exhaust system of human denial. Tears wash away the impurities of our failures. An elder once told me: "My tears say that my soul has heard something about the Other World."

3. **Earth**: Earth symbolizes the mother on whose lap everybody finds a home. The Earth person takes care of others. Earth people, like grandmothers, want all people to feel fed, content, respected and loved. According to Dagara custom, men build the structure of a house and women bring them alive.

4. **Mineral**: Mineral is elemental energy that allows us to remember. In Dagara physiology, our bones, not our brains, are the storage place of memory. In the West, we have a saying: "I knew it in my bones", which refers to a deeper, more elemental knowing than is possible through rational thought. I wonder if those in Silicon Valley, who shave stones to their essence and put them in machines of memory, already know that stones have always managed information. Perhaps the modern world's fascination with the internet can be traced to this

vast memory gap. Indigenous people don't look outside themselves they look within. Mineral people are story tellers. Their gift to society is that of remembering, through words and stories, one's origins and purpose.

5. **Nature**: Nature signifies change. It is plants and animals and landscapes. It is situated in the east opposite minerals in the west. It invites us to welcome change. The magic we crave and our attraction to the supernatural are nature in their essence. The tree, the plant, the landscape and the serpentine river zigzagging downhill on its way to the ocean, are all golden hieroglyphs capable of bringing understanding. Elevated areas function like antennae, relaying and downloading information from far away. Waterways take this information to the underworld. Barren, flat landscapes emit a fast-moving energy that is dangerous to isolated individuals. Only medicine men and women venture into wide open places at night. In heavily forested areas the trees shelter human beings from the Other World. However, at night tall trees emit a mysterious energy that may affect people's psyches as well as their bodies. That leaves the Savannah as the ideal place for the Dagara. Sandwiched between two highly charged entities, it is a natural refuge.

(http://www.englishwordplay.com/healingwisdom.htm)

Chapter 4

The True Number Line

The True Number Line is a number system created and received by AcharYah: Ausar Selassie Neteru by the Universe. It is a way to understand the vibrational frequency of all human beings on different levels using integers from -10 to +10. Each number is associated with a personality type describing that frequency level of a human being and where they are in their level of consciousness. The lowest level being "Narcissist" at negative ten to the highest level being "Convergence" at positive ten. I really connected to this number line because it made it easy to understand myself in the different stages of my life and the other people that were in my life during these stages.

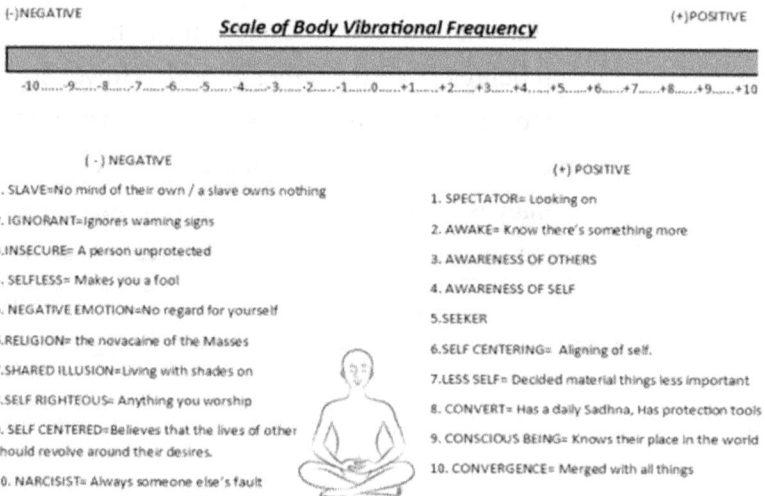

(-)NEGATIVE

Scale of Body Vibrational Frequency

(+)POSITIVE

-10.....-9.....-8.....-7.....-6.....-5.....-4.....-3.....-2.....-1.....0.....+1.....+2.....+3.....+4.....+5.....+6.....+7.....+8.....+9.....+10

(-) NEGATIVE

1. SLAVE=No mind of their own / a slave owns nothing
2. IGNORANT=Ignores warning signs
3. INSECURE= A person unprotected
4. SELFLESS= Makes you a fool
5. NEGATIVE EMOTION=No regard for yourself
6. RELIGION= the novacaine of the Masses
7. SHARED ILLUSION=Living with shades on
8. SELF RIGHTEOUS= Anything you worship
9. SELF CENTERED=Believes that the lives of other should revolve around their desires.
10. NARCISIST= Always someone else's fault

(+) POSITIVE

1. SPECTATOR= Looking on
2. AWAKE= Know there's something more
3. AWARENESS OF OTHERS
4. AWARENESS OF SELF
5. SEEKER
6. SELF CENTERING= Aligning of self.
7. LESS SELF= Decided material things less important
8. CONVERT= Has a daily Sadhna, Has protection tools
9. CONSCIOUS BEING= Knows their place in the world
10. CONVERGENCE= Merged with all things

Figure 5: True Number Line

In basic mathematics, a number line is a straight line that serves as a review of the succession of variables known as points. Every point on a number line corresponds to a specific value. The Human Species may be broken into categories with variables exhibited on a number line. Each of these variables represents a specific set of personality characteristics and values associated with their respective points on the number line. The points on the number line are represented by numbers. (Neteru, 2016, pg. 50-51)

What is interesting is that a human being can shift from level to level depending on who they associate with and who they choose to give their Qi or Chi to. Qi is vibrant energy that is held to animate the body within and is of essential importance in some Eastern systems of medical treatment such as acupuncture, and of Martial Science or self-defense such as Tai Chi. In short, Qi is basically the Human Life Force. The number line shows how we have evolved and grew throughout our lives and how trauma affects us. Our reaction to each trauma is connected to our vibrational frequency. Our ability to survive and handle each trauma without the traditional visits to a psychiatrist or psychologist, and without the traditional drugs for depression, is also related to vibrational frequency. Whether you are a Sentient Being, Conscious Being or Ascended Master, your associations can shift your energy system and either add or subtract from you.

Selassie Neteru uses addition of integers to show how the connection of two people can be affected. For example, "Remember the number line, because at this loving and

important part of the journey to Consciousness, a positive 3 (+3) can become Shared Illusion (-7) when synced with a Narcissist (-10)." (Neteru, 2016, pg. 59-60). I would like to take it a step further. As a Math Teacher, I am very familiar with the rules of integers. I have had to teach it for many years.

When adding integers, when the signs are either both negative or both positive, you combine the numbers, or add them together and keep the sign of the numbers. However, if the sign of the numbers is different, we take the difference of the two numbers, and use the sign of the larger number. For example, -5 + 8 = 3. The five is negative and the eight is positive. So, the difference between five and eight is three. The result is a positive three because the eight is larger than the five. When we change the signs and get 5 + (-8) = -3; the three becomes negative because the result will always be the sign of the larger number. When subtracting, we teach that subtracting a negative is equivalent to adding. This is due to the rule when it comes to multiplying integers. You see, multiplication is just repeated addition. When referencing multiplication with human beings, we typically mean having children. "Be fruitful and multiply" is mentioned several times in the Holy Bible: It is mentioned twice in Genesis Chapter one. Genesis 1:22 says, "And God blessed them, saying, **Be fruitful, and multiply**, and fill the waters in the seas, and let fowl multiply in the earth." Genesis 1:28, "And God blessed them, and God said unto them, **Be fruitful, and multiply**, and replenish the earth, and subdue it: and have dominion over the fish of the sea, and over the fowl of the air, and over every living thing that moveth upon the earth." It is mentioned again in Genesis Chapters Eight and Nine. Genesis 8:17 says, "Bring forth with thee every living thing that is with thee, of all flesh, both of fowl, and of cattle, and of every

creeping thing that creepeth upon the earth; that they may breed abundantly in the earth, and **be fruitful, and multiply** upon the earth. Genesis 9:1, "And God blessed Noah and his sons, and said unto them, **Be fruitful, and multiply,** and replenish the earth." This quote is mentioned again in Genesis chapter 35: Genesis 35:11, "And God said unto him, I am God Almighty: **be fruitful and multiply**; a nation and a company of nations shall be of thee, and kings shall come out of thy loins." The rules for integers change when we multiply them. So, I wondered how this would affect us as humans and our vibrational frequency if we multiplied with someone who was either on the positive or negative side of the True Number Line.

The multiplication of two positive integers is just a larger positive integer. The multiplication of two negative numbers becomes positive. But instead of seeing it as a positive symbol, I see it as a cross. A cross is the symbol of crucifixion, which is a symbol of death. The negatives cancel each other out. Two people on the negative side of the number line multiplied together equals death. Not a physical death, but a spiritual death of the vibrational frequency. In addition, when you multiply any negative number with a positive number, the result is always negative. A positive person on the number line should never multiply with a negative person on the number line. That negativity will overpower the positivity. Unlike addition, where the larger number takes the sign, in multiplication, the negative always wins no matter how big or small the number is. It would appear that negativity in this sense is more powerful than positivity. The Human psyche tends to gravitate easier toward negative emotion and negative thoughts versus the positive. There is an entire market out there geared toward helping Human Beings be positive and change their mindset from a

negative one to a positive one. It became a national interest when a documentary called "The Secret" came out in 2006. The original concept was written by Rhonda Byrne, starring Bob Proctor, Joe Vitale, John Assaraf and many others who have gone on to continue to prosper from this idea. "The Secret" consisted of interviews with leading authors, philosophers, scientists with an in-depth discussion describing The Law of Attraction on a basic scale.

After watching this documentary, I started to focus on my thoughts and discovered that most of my thoughts were negative. I would challenge that this is the case with many of us. I still have to "work" at being positive. I am still training my mind to stay positive. There are hundreds of self-help books; motivational speakers and programs geared towards helping the human being change their mentality to attract wealth, love and a healthy lifestyle. These are the three main things most humans desire. So, it makes since that when a negative is multiplied by a positive, the negative always wins.

Let's turn now to examples from my life during childhood, adolescence, young adult and adulthood that explores methods for handling trauma. In the course of our discussion we will also define Sentient Beings, Conscious Beings and Ascended Masters. You see, I believe that it is possible for a person to represent each of these at different times of their life. For example, a person born a Sentient Being could evolve into an Ascended Master. A born Ascended Master could fall victim to the social fantasies of this world and allow themselves to be ruled by Ego, therefore living the life of a Sentient Being. I will argue that the significance to realizing your true purpose is to face your trauma head on and deal with it. I will also argue that

the key to surviving traumatic experiences where they do not define you and control your life is Psycho-energetic counseling versus the traditional methods of dealing with trauma. As a Sentient Being, I reacted and responded to life primarily using the five senses. As a Conscious Being, I was more aware and was able to go deeper into my insight. The third argument is that of an Ascended Master, who usually has super abilities or comes from a family with super abilities.

Part II: Sentient Being

Sentient Beings are those who are capable of experiencing suffering and who operate using the five senses: see, touch, smell, hear and taste. They suffer from approval addiction and live life based on fate versus destiny, which means they are ruled by the ego.

> Egocentricity leads to a frozen state of Consciousness, identifying success with the repetitive stimulation of its host through materialism, carnality, and approval addiction gratified by short term and/or unauthentic praise. What I am saying here is that the ego never gets enough. No matter how much money, sex, or status we achieve the ego constantly tells us we need more. This means the ego motivates us to strive to gain and hold on to temporary happiness based on possession rather than eternal joy based on self-actualization and spiritual balance. (Neteru, 2010. pg. 26)

Sentient Beings live their life based on materialism. When they look out, they don't look out at the spiritual nature of things. They look out at the basic, sensual nature of everything. For example, a paycheck is not energy being distributed, it is how many dollars and cents are on the paycheck. A relationship is based upon: Am I physically pleased? Is this economically advantageous for me? Do you make me feel how I want to feel? Not, are we connecting on a higher plane? They think and react based on their value system. There is a selfishness deep inside that makes them think that something will be taken from them

when others try to help them. It is hard for them to trust. They are ruled by fear; therefore, they cannot grow or evolve. Their mindset is: 'It's my way or no way." If you don't do what they want, then you are the bad guy. The biggest difference between Sentient beings and Masters is that Masters ask questions; we discern; we think about how each decision we make will make us feel in the future and how it will make others feel that I may not be responsible for, but they will have an effect or impact.

It is believed by many that those who suffer from mental disorders and/or depression can benefit from consistent visits to a psychiatrist who administers medication versus energetic counseling that uses spiritual technologies and energy healing. However, from my research, I found that using FDA approved medication to numb the senses into fooling the mind that it is healed only prolongs the issues and does not heal them. Spiritual counseling focuses on getting to the root of each trauma and healing the spirit. As before mentioned, there are three main types of human beings and each type is affected by emotional trauma in a different way. The first type is the Sentient Being, who are approval addicts and believe that their life is based on fate. The nemesis to Universal Consciousness is the Corporate Ego. This universal ego attacks each type of person in a different way. A sentient being who has suffered great trauma will have a blocked energy system that hinders them from living a balanced life. This energy system consists of 7 main chakras that need to be balanced in order for a person to begin to heal. Knowing your energy type and emotional type can help each Being start the steps to healing.

Therapy and medication will not be sufficient in getting to the root of the trauma where a Sentient Being will no longer need either one. Many medications have multiple side effects

that will aid in blocking the energy system, discouraging from any real healing to take place. It is more financially beneficial for psychiatrists to never completely heal a patient. The Sentient Being naturally seeks spiritual healing. "Human Beings innately seek a spiritual path that brings about Peace, Harmony and Balance for all creation. In order to experience this, we must be willing to let go of previous conclusions that we have reached about the meaning of life received through our mental programming in the Social Fantasy" (Neteru, 2013, pg. 8). Through psycho energetic counseling, discovering and dealing with past traumas, a Sentient Being can begin to heal and apply spiritual technologies to maintain a healthy balanced emotional system.

Chapter 5

My Childhood

I was born the third of four children to an English teacher and Baptist Minister. My father pastored the churches we attended, so we were a "first family." Because of this, our family was constantly under a microscope and our every move judged. Before me, my mother had a daughter in 1970, a son in 1973 and I was born in 1975. Connections to my father have defined who I became in many ways. First, my name was picked out while my mother was still pregnant with my bother. You see, ultrasounds were only performed during emergencies and not to find out the sex of the baby. So, my mother did not know the sex of her children before they were born. A boy name and girl name would be picked out for each pregnancy. My name was selected when my father visited Denmark and met a woman he ministered to named, "Kirsten", meaning "follower of the anointed." He loved the name and knew his next daughter would have this name. His wife was pregnant, and if she was having a boy, he would be a junior, but a girl would have this unique name, which was derived from "Christian." This would have been my brother's name if he would have been a girl. So, the name was saved for me. Our names were important to my father and he was not fond of nick names. It was also important that my name was pronounced properly, so I grew up correcting people. It was a very rare name at the time.

Aside from my name, my father gave me his bow-legs and a shared illness from birth. I was born with Pyloric Stenosis,

a condition that affects the gastrointestinal tract during infancy. I was my mother's biggest baby according to my birth weight of 8 pounds and 13 ounces. It appeared that I was healthy until I started losing weight and vomiting forcefully and often, which caused other problems such as dehydration and salt and fluid imbalances. Immediate treatment for pyloric stenosis is extremely important.

> Pyloric stenosis is a narrowing of the pylorus, the lower part of the stomach through which food and other stomach contents pass to enter the small intestine. When an infant has pyloric stenosis, the muscles in the pylorus have become enlarged and cause narrowing within the pyloric channel to the point where food is prevented from emptying out of the stomach. Also called infantile hypertrophic pyloric stenosis, pyloric stenosis is a form of gastric outlet obstruction, which means a blockage from the stomach to the intestines. Pyloric stenosis is fairly common — it affects about 3 out of 1,000 babies in the United States. It's about four times more likely to occur in firstborn male infants and also has been shown to run in families — if a parent had pyloric stenosis, then an infant has up to a 20% risk of developing it. Pyloric stenosis occurs more commonly in Caucasian infants than in babies of other ethnic backgrounds. (http://kidshealth.org/en/parents/pyloric-stenosis.html)

I had surgery when I was two weeks old to correct this, which left me with a huge scar across my stomach. My father had the exact same scar. This was my first traumatic experience. Although I have no memory of it, it still affected my energy system. My root chakra was now closed.

I was born in Tyler, Texas where my father was the pastor of True Vine Baptist Church. We lived in a big, two-story house directly across the street from the church. Soon after my third birthday, my mother gave birth to a baby girl. Soon after her birth in 1978, my father was offered to pastor the oldest Black Baptist church in Texas, located in Houston. He accepted, and we moved.

Figure 6: 1975 Baby Picture, Kirsten Westbrook; sister Elicia Westbrook (left); Brother John Westbrook Jr. (right)

Antioch Missionary Baptist Church was the center of a small black residential and commercial area after the Civil War. The congregation had been founded by freed slaves in 1866, as the first black Baptist church in Houston. Richard Allen, a church member and Reconstruction representative in the Texas Legislature, built a one-story frame structure for the church at this site in 1875-1879. The Rev. John Henry Yates, a slave born in Virginia and brought to Texas by his owner during the Civil War, moved to Houston shortly after the 1865 emancipation. He became the church's first full-time pastor. The church was enlarged to its present size in 1894.(http://www.waymarking.com/waymarks/WM1Z DT_Antioch_Missionary_Baptist_Church_Houston_Te xas)

Figure 7: Antioch Missionary Baptist Church; Houston, Texas

It was a great honor for our family to be asked to pastor such an historical church. And because of the impact my father had, our family will always be remembered.

Figure 8: Rev. John Hill Westbrook, Sr.

Westbrook became pastor of historic Antioch Missionary Baptist Church in downtown Houston in 1979. During his four years of service at the church, the congregation swelled from 600 to 3,500 members. According to historian T. Berry, people came from all around to hear Westbrook's powerful sermons. (Werner, 2016, pg. 2C)

I understood at a young age how important our family was and that we were being watched and judged. I saw my mother undergo much ridicule for something as simple as what we were wearing, what she was wearing, or not behaving like a "first family." I could see her stress. I could feel her stress. I could also see and feel how my father was making history and changing lives. When I started school, I knew expectations were high, and I had to do well.

Figure 9:My father and I; age one year old.

My father was hardly home, but my mother took great care of us. I had a strong connection to my father, when he was away, I missed him greatly. At this stage of our lives we are not really sure what is real and what is not. Our minds perceive and without guidance we can block ourselves. I felt as though I was lost and no one really cared. This was primarily a struggle for identity which reflects back to my root chakra being blocked as I discussed earlier. I remember kneeling at the foot of my bed, hands clasped, head bowed, eyes closed and praying to get hurt so that I could be seen. What happened to me next will give you an idea of how powerful the subconscious mind is even when misguided.

One day during the Summer of 1983, I was playing Batman and Robin with my brother in his room. We were jumping on the bed. I got tired and laid down, while he continued to jump. His jumping caused my head to bounce up and down like a basketball. I wanted him to stop jumping, so I tripped him. He fell flat on my left arm. I jumped up and grabbed it, holding it to my chest. The pain was unbearable. He begged me not to tell as I cried, "it's broken!"

He said, "move your wrist."

And I moved my wrist back and forth.

"You see, it's just a sprang. If it was broke, you wouldn't be able to move your wrist," he exclaimed breathing heavily.

I did not want my brother to get into trouble, but I knew my arm needed assistance. I walked slowly in the living room, crying and explaining to my mother and father what happened. It was late, so my father said that he would take me to the clinic first thing in the morning. I slept that night with my arm held close to my chest. If it moved, the sharp pain vibrated throughout my entire arm. That morning, my father and I went to the clinic. The ulna, the larger bone of the forearm, was broke in two. It was a clean break. I was shocked and remembered my prayer for attention, for identity.

Though my intention came from a mindset not in my best interest and a blocked chakra, there I was, just me and my Daddy. The power of your mind will bring you what you want even if what you want is not in your best interest. They had to give me a shot that left me in and out of consciousness, but I remember my father having to carry me from room to room and then to the car. It felt so good in his arms. I did not care about the broken arm. I was just grateful I was getting this private time with my father. I never told anyone that I prayed for this. It was my secret between me and God. That was the last time I had time alone with my father.

Later that year, it was the first day of Christmas Break, December 17, 1983. I woke up after sleeping late on Saturday morning to the sounds of Saturday morning cartoons. I climbed out of bed and went to the living room to find my brother and little sister watching TV, while my older sister rummaged through the kitchen. My mother was not there, but my father was sitting comfortably in his favorite chair. I was happy to see him because his schedule as a pastor kept him away from home. He had recently had surgery on his back, so I figured that was why he was home. I enjoyed my father's time as he played games with us, telling each of us what we would be good at in life. I remember he told me that I would always have good ideas. This revelation helped me to trust my own thoughts. This time was rare, and I was highly appreciative of it. After talking to us, he went to play the organ and sang. Aside from preaching, my father loved to sing. He played the trumpet, cornet, piano and organ. My mother was also very musical, and they passed these traits on to us. I had not heard my father sing at home in a long time, so I paused from watching the movie that was on. We were watching "If You Could See What I Hear," with Shari Belafonte

and Marc Singer. My attention was drawn to the music coming from our living room. Then it suddenly stopped.

As I sat on our shag red carpet, I watched my father walk slowly from the living room to the den. He was headed for his favorite chair that sat on the far-right side of the den. It was wooden with a brown and tan leafy, floral print. Right before he reached his chair, he fell. My father was a big man, standing over six feet tall and weighing over 300 pounds. He started coughing lightly and it seemed like he was trying to get back up. He was asking for water. I sat there stunned, not knowing if he was joking or playing a prank or if he was really hurt. My oldest sister was already in the kitchen, so my brother yelled for her to bring water. She hurried out of the kitchen, dropped to her knees and put the clear cup to his mouth. The water just rolled out of the sides of his mouth as he began coughing again. More water spilled, and she was unsuccessful. My brother grabbed the phone sitting on the coffee table and dialed "0." There was no 911 in 1983. He told the operator we needed an ambulance. I was so proud that he knew what to do. And I was terrified at the look of pain in my father's eyes. The ambulance arrived minutes before my mother. They came through the front door and my mother came in through the back. We were all standing on the far-left side of the room in front of the stairs as we watched my mother rush in, drop her bags and kneel by her husband. She looked up at us and yelled for us to go upstairs and stay out of the way. The paramedics were setting up the gurney as my mother held my father's head in her lap, rocking him. I ran upstairs like I was told and stopped at the top. I dropped, and I prayed for God to help my father. He answered my prayers before. Surely, he would listen this time as well. After praying, I snuck down and peered from the corner of the stairs to see if God was answering my prayers of helping my father. I saw my father look into my mother's eyes and say, "Paula, pray, I'm dying." Then a small breath left his dry lips, and his head drooped to the side. The two men were struggling to get him on the gurney due to his size, and now that he was unconscious, it was even harder. They finally got him on and rushed him out the front door.

I knew that I just witnessed my father pass away, although there was some hope of him regaining consciousness. The whole air changed when his breath left. I felt a chill. The room felt still like time stopped. My chest was tight like my heart was sinking inside my body. That moment was forever etched in my mind. My chest still gets tight when I get upset or in a traumatic situation. When this happens like that day the air in my environment changes or if there is a change in the air quality asthma ensues. I am learning to overcome this by healing and releasing this event from my subconscious mind. In order to do this, I must delve deeper into my energy relationship with my father which actually has never ended.

Later that night, my fear was confirmed. I vaguely remember what happened from that moment up until the moment we were told. I know we stayed with neighbors. My next memory is of my siblings and I sitting on our couch in the den. A Deacon and family friend were there, along with my mother and a few other people. He told us that our father passed away.

"Ya'll have a seat. Come on, sit down," with sadness and emptiness in his eyes, he continued, "you know your daddy went to the hospital?" We all just looked at him and silently nodded our heads. "Well, he was unconscious, and they could not wake him up. Your daddy passed away."

I felt stiff on the inside and today that moment still creates chiropractic challenges in my body. I knew by their demeanor and how my mother avoided eye contact with us that it was bad news. He went on to say it was natural causes. There was a blood clot in his lungs. My Daddy was only 36 years old. Being only 8, I did not realize how young that was at the time.

Figure 10: My family: Father, Rev. John Westbrook Sr. (top left) holding baby sister, Elizabeth Westbrook; Mother, Paulette Westbrook (top right); Brother John Westbrook Jr. (bottom left); Sister, Elicia Westbrook (bottom right); Kirsten Westbrook (center)

Family can contribute to the fear of being alone through abandonment and/or death. The death of my father made me develop a fear to try certain things personally. This was the first traumatic experience I remember, but the second one that greatly affected my root chakra as well:

> This Chakra is closely linked to our primal instinct, incorporating our fundamental needs for shelter, food, and security- in short, our survival instinct. If we do not receive proper nourishment, if our needs for love, trust, and care are not met as children this Chakra will not develop properly. (Neteru, 2010, pg. 101)

What is interesting about the human psyche in this case is that my perception of my needs being met was not the intention of my mother. She was my main caretaker, along with family, school teachers and the daycare owner. They all loved me and cared for me, but I did not feel loved from them. Or maybe I just did not accept it. I felt love from my father whenever he was around. With the others, I felt forgotten. I felt they focused on my siblings or loved my siblings more than me. So, the death of my father was like the death of my love. Therefore, my Root Chakra did not develop properly.

**Figure 11: (L-R)1983 Kirsten Westbrook, age 8 and
Elizabeth Westbrook, age 5**

My father died when I was eight. I feel this contributed
to my fear of being alone as a child and throughout my young
adult life because it was hard for me to be by myself. I was a
social butterfly with very few true friendships. It took a long
time before I found comfort in being alone.

My fundamental need for security was lost when my father died.
My mother never remarried, and this void was never filled
during my childhood.

This one incident lead to many fears I grew up with. I
felt I had some big shoes to fill because my father was the first
Black to play football in the Southwest Conference and one of
the most prominent Baptist Pastors in the country. Thus, I grew

up fearing that I would fail and not live up to the family name. However, this fear made me work hard at everything I did, so my father could be proud. Experiencing death at a very young age and being aware that the adults in my immediate family did not make it past 70 years old, due to sickness and disease on both sides of my family, I also dreaded becoming obese. Like many families of African-American descent, diabetes, obesity and cancer were the main culprits. Growing up, death was the main thing I feared. I was afraid of becoming overweight, so I stayed active in sports and tried to eat healthy.

Being the middle child of four in a single parent home, I struggled with getting the attention I needed from my mother. I felt my mother's focus was on my only brother and my younger sister. If I had to contribute this stage of my life to a number on The True Number Line, I would say I was a Negative Three (-3), which is Insecure. I did not know who I was or even if I had a purpose. This insecurity developed as I grew up comparing the level of attention my younger sister and brother received to myself. I equated this attention to love. "Its primary cause is an acceptance of an ideology of competition followed closely by approval addiction" (Neteru 2016, pg. 60). Consequently, while I was in the fourth grade, I was left vulnerable and open to experience another traumatic event.

About two years after my father died, my best friend's mother, who were our neighbors across the street, introduced my mother to a family friend. He was nice and friendly. He was a red man with sandy brown hair. He started hanging around a lot. He would even spend the night. I liked that man once. He would play tag with me, my little sister and my best friend. When he would catch us, he would tickle us. It was a lot of fun, but sometimes his hand would rub against my private area while he

was tickling me. I thought it was on accident, so I ignored it. He told me I was his favorite. There was finally someone who paid attention to me and favored me instead of one of my siblings. My best friend was an only child, so she had no idea what it was like not getting attention. He made me feel special. He was fun- until he confused me. "The Insecure is prime rib for the Narcissist who loves to use their insecurity to control and manipulate them. The Narcissist will carefully observe the personal characteristics of people to determine and exploit their insecurities" (Neteru 2016, pg. 61). This man observed my need for attention and my insecurities and used them against me.

One night, he volunteered to babysit me because I was sick, and my family had a church obligation. We were sitting on the couch watching scary movies "Amityville Horror" – all three came on back to back. I was not supposed to watch scary movies, but he let me. He said it would be our secret. He sat really close to me and held me tight, as if he was protecting me. But it was uncomfortable. It was just too close. There was a bite on my thigh that kept itching. It was bothering me. He said he could help. He went and got Vaseline; but he did not fix anything. He told me I had to remove my shorts, so he could reach the bite. I just listened and complied. He started rubbing the Vaseline on my thighs, and then his hand went higher and went inside my underwear. I squirmed and tried to move away. He grabbed my arm and told me to relax. He continued to touch me on my privates and told me not to tell. I knew it was wrong and I felt alone and dirty. I felt sick to my stomach. I could not get away from his grip. This was not the man I thought I knew. I knew then that when he tickled me- he touched me there on purpose. Then I wondered if he touched my friend or my sister. I slept with my mom that night. I told myself for years it was the scary

movies- the one night I had to sleep with Mama. Soon after that I did not see him anymore; perhaps my mother could sense something was wrong.

I relegated the memory of that man touching me out to my unconscious mind where it would resurface again when I was in college watching a special on pedophiles (on The Oprah Winfrey Show). The man was describing how they choose their victims; how they get close to the family, so they can be trusted with the children alone; how they gain the trust of the child, so the child is less likely to tell. As I sat there watching and listening- it all came back to me. I remembered that entire night. I never knew I was one of them- a victim- *a colored girl* that was molested. Through our neighbors, I found out that he was arrested. We later read in the paper that he robbed and killed a cab driver. He was sentenced to death and eventually died in prison.

This man showed me some much-needed attention that led to me being molested. Now my Sacral Chakra was blocked. The Sacral Chakra is associated with your sexuality, the nature of your relationships, freedom from guilt, pleasure and nurturance, sensation and creativity. Although the memory stayed blocked for many years, I suffered years of broken relationships and more trauma due to this incident.

> Swadisthana, the second Chakra, means abode of the vital force and is the center of your pleasure, creativity, sensuality, nurturance, and emotions. In other words, this powerhouse of energy has the potential to provide you with the basis to form meaningful relationships with self, and others. The ego is formed and perpetuated in these first two Chakras. (Neteru, 2010, pg. 102)

Sentient Beings depend on and rely on the Ego. So, due to these traumatic experiences early on in my life that caused my first two Chakras to close, my decisions and choices were led by my Ego, which only lead to more trauma and heartache.

Chapter 6

Adolescence

As a young girl, I wasn't very nice. In fact, I was mean. I found joy in making fun of people and I thought that I was better than most of the people around me. Talking about people was the way I protected myself from pain and getting close to anyone new. I had the same group of friends since kindergarten, so they were all I needed. I stopped trusting. Someone I trusted and cared about hurt me, so I would do and say things to push people away. When it came to "Playing the Dozens" or "choppin'" on people, I was a professional. "Playing the Dozens" was a game of words and wit. You would talk about someone and/or their family members. "Yo mama" jokes were the most popular to use. I was known for making up my own jokes that no one heard before and were personal to that individual. It was a defense mechanism; nevertheless, I did not realize how much I was really affecting others. I would make everybody laugh and people knew not to bother me if they didn't want me to talk about them. I was clever with my choice of words and if I needed to, I would hit below the belt. I was being ruled by my Ego; I was surviving. Until one day, I made fun of the wrong boy.

I was sitting in homeroom in my 6th grade class. There was a boy who I'd known since kindergarten in my class. He was popular and mischievous. But he was short.

"Look everybody, Jay's feet don't reach the floor," I said pointing at his small feet dangling above the floor. The whole class burst out in laughter.

"Shut-up, I'm sitting on my backpack," he screamed grabbing his backpack and showing the class. But it didn't matter, the class was still laughing. He looked around, getting more and more upset. He looked at me, and yelled, "That's why I'm glad yo' daddy died!" The whole class got quiet and started staring at me. I stopped laughing. I went to a dark place. For the rest of the day, I tried to avoid him. However, his anger toward me worsened when our peers kept telling him he was wrong for what he said. Later that day, while I was waiting for the bell to ring after lunch, he came up behind me and tapped me on the shoulder. When I turned around, he slapped me hard across my face, then took off running. I dropped my books and started chasing him. My face getting redder as tears rolled down my cheeks. The sting was like nothing I ever felt before. My vision was blurry from the tears and he was fast. I stopped to catch my breath. I wiped my eyes and saw a group of people dragging him my way. I could hear others yelling to tell my big brother what had happened. They dropped him in front of me. I balled up my fist and started hitting him all over until my arms got tired. Then the same group dragged him to my brother, who already stood 6 feet tall in the 8th grade. He was a star football and basketball player. Through blurred eyes, I could see this boy hanging up on the wall being held up by my brother. I was later told that my brother threatened him and instructed him to leave his sister alone. I felt proud that my brother would take up for me.

Then, the summer between my 6th grade and 7th grade year, we moved further North in the city. My safety net of friends was over. See, there were no cell phones. It was pretty much "out of sight, out of mind" for all my friends from school. I used to call some of them at first, but nobody ever called me. So, I stopped calling them. I tried to make friends with the

people who lived in our apartment complex and went to my school. I thought I was being successful until I saw a "Slam Book" with a page with my name on it. A Slam Book is a notebook (commonly the spiral-bound type) which is passed among children and teenagers. The keeper of the book starts by posing a question (which may be on any subject) and/or placing certain names at the tops of pages, and the book is then passed around for each contributor to fill in their own answer to the question and make comments about how they feel about the person whose name is at the top of the page. The comments are signed with a number instead of a name. It is supposed to be anonymous, but you sign your name next to the number in the front of the book.

Slam books were also a source of bullying between students - where students "lived in fear" of the "biting comments" written anonymously under their names, "on the order of what today might be a Tweet or a Facebook comment." Well, a Slam Book was passed to me and as I was going through it, I came across a page with my name on it. As I read the comments, my chest tightened as the cruel words stabbed me. I could feel the holes in my back as I checked the names in the front to see who hated me so much. It was "my friends" that wrote the worse comments. The most positive comment was, "she is ok." The page was full of negative remarks about how those closest to me really felt about me. This was another traumatic experience. My insecurities only grew, making me put a wall up.

In church, I was about a year older than all the other girls, so they looked up to me. Plus, our family was already well respected because of who my father was. I was pretty and athletic, and I was vain about it. It was the opposite of school,

where I felt the need to prove myself. However, I would say whatever I was thinking and not consider how it would affect those around me. Like I mentioned before, I was mean. I had no idea how bad it was until one evening I was approached. We were on a Baptist Convention in Baltimore, MD staying at the Embassy Suites Hotel. One of the girls came and got me from my room and lead me to a conference room with one chair and all the children from the church. She sat me in the chair. It was an intervention; one that would change my life forever. They each took turns explaining how my words and actions had affected them in deep ways. They described times when I made them cry and doubt themselves. I sat there wondering why my words had such an impact. I wondered why they even cared about what I said. I was the cause of their depression and they wanted me to stop.

While trying to protect myself from pain and heartache, I was causing it for others. I realized that people actually listened to me and cared about what I had to say. I knew that I had to be careful about my words. I never understood before that day how powerful words could be. I made a huge personality shift that day. I decided to be "nice." I decided to pay attention to my words and what I said. This intervention showed me how important I was and that I was not ordinary.

My Freshman year in High School, I was in my first serious relationship with a young man that was a year older. We dated for about six months, and during that time, we had a lot of fun, but he would try to pressure me to have sex. I was still a virgin and wanted to stay that way. We came close twice and I knew he would not give up, so fearing I would yield to temptation, I broke up with him. This may sound like an everyday teenage relationship, but there were deeper issues going on. During the relationship, my boyfriend suffered from depression, thoughts of suicide and had a very unhealthy relationship with his mother. I helped him get through these problems. He had two best friends that he was always with, and one of them died. My boyfriend confided in me that he did not think he would live to see the age of seventeen. Another tragedy he experienced while dating me, was the brutal murder of his brother-in-law and sister. Because I was the only good thing in his life, breaking up with him sent him down a negative spiral that eventually lead to his demise. His friends begged me to reconsider, saying that he was lost and turning dark. This was too much pressure for a fourteen-year-old girl, and I was too young to understand my power.

The neighborhood he lived in was saturated with members of a gang called Crips, and they had been pressuring him to join. While he was with me, he refused. He focused on his schoolwork, art and woodshop. He drew me pictures and made me a coat hanger with my name carved in it that I still have today. He thought of killing himself several times, but the thought of me stopped him. His need for me was too much pressure. It was scary for me. After the break-up, he joined the gang and became the son that his mother thought he was. His best friend blamed me for what was happening. Two years later, he was gunned down by police.

During those two years after the break-up, I would see him occasionally, and hear stories. None of them good. The last story I heard was that he was driving with a friend and the police began chasing them. Because they had a gun in the car, he refused to pull over and decided to try and outrun the police. The police started shooting at the car, claiming they were aiming for the tires. They shot him in the head and killed him. I was a senior

in high school when I heard about this. He had just turned 17 a month before he was killed.

I have always partially blamed myself for his passing, thinking if I stayed with him, he would still be alive. I felt like he truly loved me because he was the first boy to show me what it was like to be loved and needed, but I was not ready for that kind of love. It was terrifying for me. I did not want to end up pregnant as a teenager. Experiencing another death of someone close to me and the sexual tension further led to the blocking of my Root and Sacral Chakras. Blaming myself for another person's death also caused my Solar Plexus Chakra to close. The Solar Plexus Chakra, located about 2 inches above the navel is the core of our personality, our identity, and our ego. The third chakra is the center of willpower. While the Sacral chakra seeks pleasure and enjoyment, the third chakra is all about the perception of who you are. The gift of this chakra is sensing your personal power, being confident, responsible, and reliable. The third chakra is the center of your self-esteem, your willpower, self-discipline, as well as warmth in your personality. Feeling this level of shame and guilt as a teenager and not knowing how powerful my influence was on this young man, caused this chakra to be blocked.

High school for me, like countless others, was like a roller coaster of emotions. My second serious relationship was also in High School. I dated the same boy my Sophomore and Junior years. I can truly say I was in love with this boy. He had a pure heart, was beautiful and musically talented. He was one year older, and I loved his family. We made history together at this school.

My Sophomore year was full of new and exciting things. When we noticed that there was only one Black cheerleader and

one Black girl on the drill team, we decided to start our own thing. My friends and I started a step team called Alpha Phi Beta. We met this guy who was a member Alpha Phi Alpha fraternity at a party. We would meet at our homes and practice. He would teach us step routines. We performed these routines at the basketball games. Our colors were red and black. We had shirts made and everything. This was empowering for me. When it was getting close to February, I began to inquire about a Black History Program. Our school was known for putting on huge plays and productions, but they had never had a Black History program and did not recognize Martin Luther King Day. We did not get this day off.

After speaking with some of the Black teachers and our only Black Assistant Principal, we got permission to put on a Black History Program. One of the history teachers was over it. I spoke to my boyfriend about helping start a gospel choir due to his musical background. We also knew this family of singers that attended our school and we asked them if they would help. My friend and I went around asking people if they could sing and would they be interested. We got our choir together and started practicing after school in the gym. The choir sounded great and I was proud of our accomplishments. We were on program to open with the Negro National Anthem, "Lift Every Voice and Sing."

My step team was also on program to perform. The program was such a success and we had such a great turn out, that Mr. Spenser, the Assistant Principal, made it a permanent part of our schedule. This was also the case with the Gospel Choir. We continued these programs and the choir my Junior and Senior year. I later learned that everything continued even after I graduated, and the Gospel Choir became a part of UIL to

perform and compete against other choirs. The University Interscholastic League (UIL) is an organization that creates rules for and administers almost all athletic, music, and academic contests for public, primary and secondary schools in the American state of Texas.

I had a voice at this school. People listened to me and respected me. This was very good for my Throat Chakra, the Fifth Chakra also called, Vishuddha. The throat chakra is the voice of the body. It is a pressure valve that allows the energy from the other chakra to be expressed. Because it is the first of the three spiritual chakras, it is important for it to be balanced because if it is out of balance or blocked it can affect the health of the other chakras. Since mine was beginning to open, I could express what I thought and what I felt.

During my boyfriend's Senior year, right before Prom, he broke up with me. The reason he gave was that he did not think he could resist wanting to be intimate with me, so he needed space from the temptation. You see, he was a "good Christian boy" who wanted to wait until marriage like I did. But like most teenagers, we fooled around. I was devastated. I became emotionally withdrawn and depressed for months. I could not understand his logic, and the decision was out of the blue. My Heart Chakra was now closed, and my insecurities continued to cultivate, making me a magnet for Narcissists.

Aside from the death of my ex-boyfriend, my Senior year was quite full of ups and downs. Starting out the year, I had to make a decision concerning Track and Field. I had been running track since seventh grade, and at the end of my Junior year, my coach quit. I could not even imagine myself being coached by anyone else. I knew this was my last year to try and earn some

type of scholarship and although I was fast, I was not fast enough. I suffered an injury to my hamstring and I never really came back from that. Also, my younger sister was going into the 9th grade. She had broken all my records at the Middle School, and I was afraid that she was now faster than me. That would have been catastrophic to my reputation. So, I decided not to run track and to just focus on my grades. I was already in Honors and Advanced classes, and I was the only Black in these classes. This would turn out to be a blessing and a curse.

Figure 12: 1992 Track Season; Kirsten Westbrook, 11th Grade

Being the only Black person many of my classmates associated with, they started to feel comfortable enough to ask me questions regarding my race.

"Can I touch your hair?"

"How come a perm makes your hair straight, but it makes mine curly?"

"Why are yawl so loud?"

"If dirt is brown and you're brown, how do you know when you are clean?"

These were just a few that I can remember. Although many of the questions made me want to physically slap them, I maintained my cool, and just answered the questions:

"No, you cannot touch my hair. The perm you use and the perm I use is different. You guys are just as loud as us. We only stand out because it's just a few of us compared to you guys. Can you see the dirt on your skin? Well, neither can I. I know I'm clean the same way you do."

Because I kept my cool and did not cuss them out, they all started liking me. However, my Black classmates did not feel the same affection. I had a few friends, but most were fake. My fellow track mates developed a clique and they would all talk about me behind my back. I did not understand it then, but I later realized it was jealousy. I had never done anything to them. They would analyze my clothes, my hair or anything they could find to talk about- everyday. Despite their disdain, when Homecoming rolled around, I was nominated along with four other girls to be Homecoming Queen. The only other time a black Homecoming Queen was nominated and won was two years prior, and she was a cheerleader. I was going up against a very popular cheerleader who won everything every year. At the Homecoming game, my brother was my escort. Each candidate had their own cheering section. One girl even had shirts made. I did not have a section. It was just my mother and little sister. I stood there in a bright yellow dress and white heels with my brother on my arm as they made the announcement.

"And the 1992 Homecoming Queen for Klein Forest High School is... Kirsten Westbrook!" My brother gripped my

arm tightly as he raised his other arm with glee. I was shocked and excited as I grinned tightly from ear to ear.

Figure 13: Yearbook picture capturing my expression as my name was called for winning the 1992 Homecoming Queen for Klein Forest High School. My brother, John Westbrook, escorted me in the place of my father.

The 1991 Homecoming Queen was not there to crown me, so I was crowned by our Head Principal. He slowly approached me and placed a crown on my head. There was a group of girls that booed because their friend did not win. The Homecoming King was a star football player who was also Black. We were the first Black couple to ever win Homecoming King and Queen at Klein Forest High School. My mother did not bring a camera, so the only pictures I have are the ones the yearbook took. They let me have a few copies. When I asked my mother why she did not take pictures or tell anyone, she said, "I did not tell anyone or bring a camera because I did not think you would win." Sadly, I was not surprised. This confirmed my feeling of neglect that I had always felt from my mother. I was sure that if it had been my brother, John or sister, Elizabeth, we would have had a section blocked off just for our family and friends. As happy as I was wining, there was a sorrow that crept in when I saw the amount of support everyone else had that was on the homecoming court.

Figure 14: 1992 Homecoming Court for Klein Forest High School

Winning Homecoming Queen set a precedent for the rest of the school year. I was now more popular than I had ever been on my own. I was always in the shadow of my brother, and my popularity was due to his. Not being in athletics, I continued to study hard and make good grades. The last class of the day was study hall, led by one of the head football coaches. He was African-American and really friendly with the students (sometimes too friendly). I heard rumors that he would take a special liking to young girls, but I knew he was married with kids, so I did not want to believe this. I used this class period to do homework and get ahead of my studies. However, most of the other students just goofed off. After winning Homecoming

Queen with a Black King by my side, our peers and our teachers expected us to date. His father was a preacher and knew who my father was. And subsequently, the pressure was on.

The coach started giving me messages from the King that he wanted to ask me out but was afraid I would turn him down. There was a girl in that same class that I knew was secretly seeing the King. She was a red head and she was white. Her mother was the Librarian and did not approve of her dating him. His dark complexion bothered her. This young man was known for dating outside his race. I had never seen him with a Black girlfriend, and I think his father wanted him to date me. He assumed I only went out with light-skinned guys. So, I was being accused of being "color-struck." "Color Struck" is an old saying among African-Americans that refers to individuals who believe that a lighter complexion and European features represent the epitome of beauty and desirability. Color discrimination is often masked by a combination of subjective notions of attractiveness and unconscious stereotypes. Michael Jackson and Sammy Sosa were probably not consciously attempting to look White; it is more likely they were simply color struck.

**Figure 15: 1992 Klein Forest
Homecoming King and Queen**

I never thought of myself as such. I did not care what your complexion was. The few boyfriends I had were mostly light-skinned, but I had dark-skinned boyfriends too. I realized that most dark-skinned boys just did not approach me. To prove the King wrong, I agreed to go on a date with him. He was a gentleman, and I could tell he was raised in a good home; however, his ideals were different from mine and I knew that we would never be anything past friendship. We had a nice time, but I was not impressed with the conversation.

The next day at school, I got an ear full from the red head about our date. She was distraught. Apparently, he called her after our date and bragged about taking me out. She saw me as a threat and I told her that I was not a threat and I was not interested in him in that way. I could not understand why she was so upset.

Then I asked the question, "Did you sleep with him?"

She raised her head slowly behind teary eyes and shook her head no. Yet, all her friends behind her signaled to me that she had.

"You did. That's the problem right there. Nothing happened between us. You have nothing to worry about, and I think he's wrong for making you feel this way," I explained.

The coach was thoroughly entertained. Surprisingly, the King asked me out again. His dad made him. I agreed just so I could speak to him about the red head. Although the red head was not my friend, we had several classes together and I began counseling her about boys and especially this young man. This made me even more popular amongst the White girls. Her friends started asking me for advice as well. They respected me, but the Black girls did not.

I would hear rumors and whispers daily of something negative that was being said about me. They would laugh and giggle, pointing in my direction. It was annoying, and I pretended like it did not bother me, but it did. The main culprit was a female track star and her crew. I never understood why she hated me so much. She did not even know me. We never hung out and the only time we spoke was when she was asking for help on her English homework. Then she would slander me behind my back. I later found that my so-called best friend since 7th grade, was also a ring-leader. My little sister ran track with them, and they seemed to like her. She also took an elective class with them. I believe it was Public Speaking. They made the mistake and thought they could slander me in front of her. She annihilated them all verbally, especially my best friend.

After the mess with the King died down, the Coach started acting funny toward me. He was being extra playful. He would throw things at me. Bump me in the halls. It felt like

flirting. It made me feel very uncomfortable. I tried to ignore him, but the more I tried, the more aggressive he became. One day, during class, he kept throwing little pieces of paper at me to distract me, and I yelled for him to stop.

"Will you stop! You play too much!" I just kind of snapped. I had held in the frustration for weeks. That was my first time disrespecting or yelling at an adult. I wanted to cry. He just looked at me in shock.

As I was leaving the class, he grabbed me, "Hey, what's wrong with you?"

"Let me go," I demanded. He was holding me tightly and I knew this was not apposite behavior.

"Not until you tell me what's wrong,' he replied.

I then attempted to pull away, and in doing so I jammed my finger on the door and broke my nail. As soon I was free of his grip, I quickly walked away, getting lost in the crowd of teenagers. When I got home, my mother noticed my finger and asked me what happened. After I told her, she immediately called the school and set up a teacher conference. When my mother and I arrived, sitting in the conference room in the office was the Principal, Assistant Principal and my counselor. We took our seats and waited for the Coach, who arrived shortly after we sat down. My mother spoke and voiced her concerns. The Coach replied, admitting that he was just playing around with me and did not mean any harm. My mother, being an educator herself, reminded him of his responsibilities as a teacher and that playing with students was not one of them. She then turned to me and told me to tell him how it made me feel. I began speaking with my head lowered.

Cutting me off, my mother sternly said, "Look at me."

With discomfort, I looked at my mother, not knowing why she cut me off.

"Whenever you talk to somebody, you always look them in the eye. That is the only way they will respect you. Now look him in the eye and tell him how he made you feel."

I nodded, turned and looked the Coach square in the eye. Remembering I had a voice, I spoke with confidence as I told him how I thought his playful actions were inappropriate and immature. I explained that he made me feel uncomfortable and that I wanted to be left alone. He agreed to leave me alone and apologized for his behavior. We were then dismissed from the meeting. My mother left, and I went to class. I never forgot my mother's words. Still today, I look every person in the eye when I speak to them. I learned a valuable lesson that day about demanding respect and not being afraid to speak my mind, even if the words are not easy to say.

After that meeting, the Coach did not speak to me again, and I was happy about that. The year was coming close to an end, and the mean girl crew was in full effect. It was time for the school to nominate and vote on Senior Class Favorites for male and female. Some of the categories were: Best Athlete, Most Likely to Succeed, Funniest, Most Likely to be an Actress/Actor, Best-Dressed, and the most important one, Mr. and Miss Klein Forest.

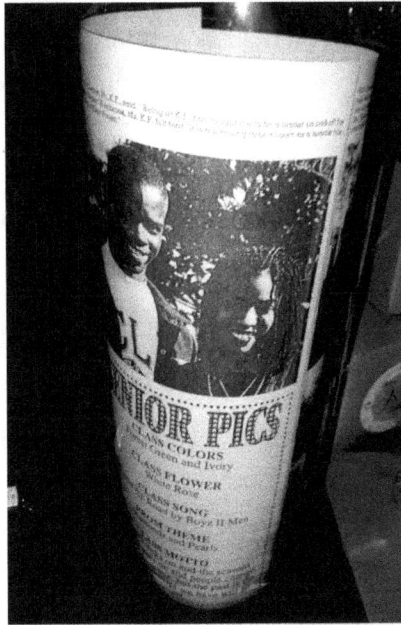

Figure 16: Copy of Yearbook Photo featuring Mr. and Miss Klein Forest

I was nominated for Miss Klein Forest. I was a little surprised, but since I had been at this school, the Homecoming court usually was the same nominees for Mr. And Miss Klein Forest. We did not have a Prom King and Queen, so many felt like this was synonymous with that. This was the only category that the entire school would vote on. All the other categories were voted on by the seniors only. We also voted on our Senior song, colors and Prom Theme. Thanks to my little sister, most of the Freshman class voted for me. That mean girl crew tried to get people to not vote for me, but it did not work. I won anyway, and the King won as Mr. Klein Forest. We were coupled once again.

It was time for Prom. I asked my mother if I could have a dress custom made. I felt it was imperative that I look exquisite. She agreed and we found a seamstress that lived nearby. She had a book of dresses and I selected a wedding dress that she said she could turn into a prom dress just by changing the colors. I selected a deep green color and black. The body and sleeves of the dress was green lace. The bottom was chiffon, and I had chiffon on the shoulders.

I did not have a boyfriend at the time, but I was crushing on a boy from church. He was going out with a sophomore that went to my school and attended our church. He liked me too, but we just remained friends. He had a cousin that was a little older and considered a "pretty boy"; he suggested I ask him. He knew that his cousin would respect me and make me look good at the same time. His cousin was flattered and agreed to be my Prom date.

Figure 17: Kirsten Westbrook with Prom date on steps of apartment.

Figure 18: 1993 Prom picture of Kirsten Westbrook

My dress was ready, and I was so excited to see it. When she pulled it out, I looked at it and thought that it did not look anything like the dress I picked. It was pretty, but the colors changing from white to black and green changed the whole look of the dress. Well, it did not matter if I liked it or not. My mother paid for it and I was going to wear it. I kept these feelings to myself. A friend of mine that lived in our apartments did my make-up. My hair was in an updo with curls coming over to the side.

Everything was going great until the mean girl crew showed up. They could not stop looking, pointing and laughing. It was so bad that their dates got upset, complaining that they were too focused on me instead of them. The track star's boyfriend was on the basketball team. I worked with the team and was cool with many of them, so he was my friend. He took up for me and I found out that they were talking about me during the ride to the prom. The focus was my dress. One of the girls had a dress very similar to mine, except it was white and she did not have sleeves. But the lace and chiffon were the same. I did my best to not pay attention to them. I was happy that the fellas had my back and realized how petty these girls were. My date was a gentleman and we had a good time.

The next week a recruiter came to the school from Texas A&M University. He asked to see a select few students of color that would qualify for an academic scholarship based on their GPA and involvement in school activities. I had already applied to the schools I wanted to go to, but I agreed to see him. It was about ten of us. My so-called best friend was one them. Another person in our meeting was another friend from middle school. She was like the mediator between me and my bestie. Whenever she would pull a cruel prank on me or plan to do something mean, this girl would give me a heads up. I would decide to stop being friends with her, but she would always come apologizing and I would always forgive her. She was a Narcissist and it was her job to throw me off my center.

Well, we were all given the applications to fill out, and we did that before the recruiter left. He submitted the applications for us and informed all three of us that we got the scholarship a few days later. It was for $10,000 spread over four years. The recruiter reminded me that I had to apply to the school. He set up a time for us to come out to the school and take a look at the campus. Since my bestie lived in my apartments and our families knew each other, we went together. The campus was huge. It was like it was a small city. We had to take a tram to get from one side of the campus to the other. The main campus is one of the largest in the United States, spanning 5,200 acres. I was disappointed that I was not going to the other schools I applied to, but was excited about this opportunity. The recruiter told us that we needed to apply for housing, and if we wanted to be roommates, we could put each other's names and Social Security numbers on the form and send it in at the same time. We both agreed.

The deadline for housing was getting near and I had not heard from my bestie. I needed her information to put on my application. I asked her about it, and she told me that she got a Track scholarship to the University of Texas for more money and decided to go there. I was disappointed and upset because sending in my paperwork late would mean that I could get anything. I should not have been surprised though. This was her norm.

With one week of school left, they made an announcement that if any senior had a fight, that they could not walk across the stage during graduation. I did not worry about this because I was not the type to get into fights. But little did I know, there was a plan brewing to set me up. I was walking down the hall, and two of the mean girls were in front of me. They did not see me, but I could hear them. They were slandering me and talking about how ugly my prom dress was.

"It's amazing how much you guys think about me. I don't think about you at all. Why are you worried about what I'm wearing," I said snickering behind them.

"A'int nobdy worried about you!" the track star screamed. She then tried to come at me, but was hesitant. Her friend started holding her and pulling her toward the stairs. "You better be glad she holding me back! Watch your back!" she yelled turning around.

I just kept laughing at their ignorance, but then I remembered that announcement and realized how close I was to getting into a fight. If she had hit me, I would have hit her back. I decided to go straight to the Assistant Principal and use that voice I learned I had.

"Hello Mr. Spencer, can I speak with you?" approaching him in his office.

"Sure, Kirsten. What can I do for you?" He answered.

"There are a group of girls possibly planning to jump me. If anybody hits me, I am going to hit them back. That's how I was raised. My daddy told me if somebody hits me, to hit them back even harder. But believe me when I tell you, I am going to walk across that stage. I am the only Black person in the top ten percent. That should count for something. I am letting you know what is going on, and I need you to have my back if anything happens to make sure I walk across that stage." I looked him square in the eye the whole time I spoke.

Figure 19: 1993 Senior Graduation Photo of Kirsten Westbrook

"I see. You don't have anything to worry about. Who are these girls?" He asked.

"Come on, Mr. Spencer, you know who they are. Just make sure I walk, ok? I gotta get to class. Can you write me a pass?" It was a well-known fact that these girls did not like me. I did not think it was necessary to name drop.

"Thank you for letting me know. And yes, I am very proud of everything that you have done here at this school. Here is your pass." He handed me the pass with a smile, and I headed to English.

The rest of the day I was looking over my shoulder, but nothing happened. I did not even see them the rest of the day. It was weird, but I was satisfied and proud of myself for speaking to the Assistant Principal. I later found out that my sister threatened them and told them she had nothing to lose because she was changing schools. She let them know that she would beat them down if they even tried to touch me. She had my back once again. Although she was a Freshman, she had their respect because she proved herself on the track. She could outrun them all. I also later found out the reason the track star hated me so much was because of her boyfriend. Based on some comments he made, she thought that we liked each other; but we were just friends.

Figure 20: Kirsten Westbrook at Award Ceremony receiving chords and collar for being in the National Honor Society and Top 10% of Graduating class.

I graduated Summa Cum Laude with a Grade Point Average of 4.2 and was the first Black to walk across that stage. Summa Cum Laude means With Highest Praise or With Highest Honor. I was on my way to Texas A&M University on an academic scholarship. The irony is that I never applied to this school originally. I applied to Hampton University, Howard University, Spellman University and Xavier University- all Historically Black Colleges/ Universities. My High School was predominantly white, and I wanted a change. I got into all those other schools, but with no way to pay for them, I had to go to Texas A&M. About two weeks before I was to go to school, I received my information of where I would be staying on campus. It was a dorm called Rudder. Two days later, I got a phone call from a friend. I don't even remember who called, but I remember the conversation.

"Hey girl, you still going to Texas A&M?"

"Yea, I leave in about two weeks."

"Who's your roommate going to be?"

"I don't know; I have her name, but I don't know her."

"Yea, your bestie is going too. I just spoke to her."

"What? Naw, she told me she was going to UT on a track scholarship."

"Nope, she's going to A&M, and guess who's her roommate?"

She told me that her roommate was the same friend that was like a mediator. I was stunned and felt more betrayed than ever. They both just lied straight to my face. How evil can you be? I was so hurt. This was the last bit of drama I was going to allow this girl to put me through, and I could not believe my other friend. After years of her helping me dodge her antics, she was now a part of it. I made a decision to cut them both off.

Chapter 7

College

If High School was a roller coaster of emotions, college was the *Kingda Ka* at Six Flags Great Adventure, standing 456 ft. tall in Jackson, New Jersey- the tallest roller coaster in the United States. Despite my trauma, I was ready for college and excited about being away from home. Texas A&M in 1993 had a Black student population of 2.5% and 0.5% Black faculty.

At this point in my life, I am still a Sentient Being with a Vibrational Frequency of Negative Three, which is Insecure, meaning unprotected. Sadly, this was only the foundation of my pain. This learned fear led to a phobia of being afraid of the unknown under the value system influenced by relationships. There was a time when I was very trusting of people and looked forward to getting to know new people and make new friends. The next years of my life, I will experience suffering like none other, coupled with a breakthrough that had me question my religion and faith.

College started out pretty good. I was enthusiastic to be away from home and on my own. My major was Political Science because I wanted to be an Attorney, but Texas A&M did not have a pre-law degree program. I was told that majoring in Political Science would help prepare me for law school. I loved my dorm. Rudder was the newest dorm on the North side of the campus. My room was like a hotel room. I had one roommate and we had our own bathroom. I was surprised because I turned in my paperwork so late. I eventually ran into those girls from high school and I totally ignored them. I learned

that they stayed on the South side of campus in an older dorm with community bathrooms. That was true karma. My roommate was white and seemed shocked that I was not. She thought I was by looking at my name. I started making friends right away, many of whom I am still in touch with. It was seven of us.

Figure 21: (L-R back row) Kayce, Monika and Temetria; (center) Sunnye; (L-R front row) Kirsten, Kim and Rabiyyah

We called ourselves "The Freshman Crew." We were a group of pretty, smart females who agreed to have each other's backs. We were well-known amongst the Black students. The hangout spot was The Commons, where the Northside cafeteria was, and had a dorm attached. All seven of us stayed on the Northside of campus. Four of the girls all graduated from

Willowridge High School in Houston: Kayce, Sunnye, Kim and Rabiyyah. Temetria was from Fort Worth and Monika was from Humble. There were five guys a part of our crew as well. Out of the five, two were dating myself and Kim. Victor was also from Houston and Herb was Kim's boyfriend.

Victor was intriguing. He was a "bad boy" who escaped the gang life to go to college. He had a huge scar on his face from being in a knife fight. I thought he was cute, really cool and that he made a great choice to turn his life around. Our relationship did not last long because he accused me of cheating on him with an upperclassman that was a member of Alpha Phi Alpha Fraternity.

He was truly wrong. I was approached by an Alpha, but not for that reason. The Miss Black and Gold Scholarship Pageant, under the sponsorship of Alpha Phi Alpha Fraternity, Inc., is an outgrowth of the long tradition of Alpha Chapters' designation of outstanding young ladies to serve as "Chapter Sweethearts." This Alpha was asking me to participate in the pageant. Throughout the history of Alpha Phi Alpha Fraternity, Inc. the Miss Black and Gold Scholarship Pageant has become very near and dear to the hearts of Alpha men and this chapter. The Pi Omicron Chapter of Alpha Phi Alpha were looking for ladies who exemplify the beauty, intelligence, and poise worthy of a scholarship.

I was honored that I was even thought of, and I gave it much thought. I decided to do it. The scholarship money could help since the scholarship I had did not cover all costs. The scholarship money would be spread across the winner, first runner up, second runner up and miss congeniality. The scoring was over the following categories: Judges Interview; Achievements and Projection; Fashion Show (replaced

Swimwear); Creative and Performing Arts; Oral Expression, Poise and Appearance and Scholarship. The Judges Interview was a ten-minute interview in front of a panel of judges where each of them asked me a different question. I was judged on my sense of values and perception and concern in human relations. For the Achievements and Projection portion, we had to give a small 90 second speech introducing ourselves to the audience, highlighting our accomplishments. The Fashion Show was collective, but we were looked at individually. Years prior, it was Swim Wear, but due to complaints of the girls being too exposed, they changed it to a Fashion Show. We were judged on posture and poise. Creative and Performing Arts was our talent that had to be performed within three minutes. Scoring was based on originality, technical ability, costume and stage presence. The Oral Expression, Poise and Appearance portion was the response to one question on current events while wearing an Evening gown and being escorted by one of the gentleman in the Fraternity. This was the last presentation piece. The Scholarship portion was based on our academic achievements and GPA from the previous semester.

I felt confident that I could do this because I participated in a pageant about a year prior that had over 100 contestants and I was in the top 20. This pageant would only have about 10-15 contestants. My prize for being in the top 20 of that pageant was free modeling school. I started modeling at Barbizon Modeling School in Houston during the summer before I went off to college. I went home every weekend to continue.

After submitting my paperwork, I was chosen as a finalist to be in the pageant along with 11 other girls. The pageant was scheduled for the end of January in 1994. We had to come back early from Christmas break to prepare and learn our dance routine. Luckily, I had my own entourage of helpers. My six girlfriends helped me tremendously to prepare. For my talent, I decided to do Spoken Word Poetry. I wrote poetry myself, but my brother had a poem that I loved, and I thought that it would make a great performance piece. However, it was controversial. The title was "Asiatic Intelligence, Black Ignorance."

I was really enjoying my experience and was excited about the pageant. However, I noticed when we would go through our presentations and talents, there was one contestant that would do something different each time. She was a Senior and a member of a sorority. I developed close relationships with my pageant sisters, but a few of them seemed really egotistical. The day of the pageant, I was ready. However, when I did my Judge Interview, I noticed one of the judges was an older white male. This worried me because of the poem I was going to do for my talent could be considered insulting. I just hoped that he would not mark me too low. Each time I got on that stage, I was confident and engaged the audience. I received three standing ovations and was the only one to get so many.

The one category that I felt weak in was the one where I did not have much control. We were partnered up for the Fashion Show portion and my partner chose our outfits. It was denim and loose fitting. In other words, boring. I knew from going to Modelling school, to have multiple items to remove and twirl around added flare to your walk. I was not able to be there when the girls picked the outfits. The young lady I mentioned earlier picked a black leather outfit that accented her curves, with several accessories, including a hat. And she showed out and stood out. I had to give it to her. I also noticed that when she did her talent, her music and entire routine was different from what

she showed us in rehearsal. She tap-danced. But I thought the dance was boring and the audience did not even pay attention.

It was time to announce the winners. I felt very confident that I would at least place due to the amount of love I received from the audience. To my dismay, I did not get anything. They announced that the first five girls' scores were extremely close by only a tenth of a point. and you can guess that the young lady I mentioned won the whole thing. When they called her name, the audience booed, and I wanted to cry. Then, one of the judges came out of the booth onto the stage to embrace the winner. I later learned that they were sorority sisters. This pageant was rigged. I was upset and felt betrayed. I put so much work into everything that I did and was proud of myself.

Although I did not win, I made a name for myself and became one of the most popular Freshman at the school. During the following weeks, I was approached by various people saying they thought I should have won and that I was the best one by far. They agreed that the contest was rigged. Of course, the brothers of the Fraternity denied such accusations and maintained that the scores were really close. When I saw how that young lady cheated, I lost complete respect for that sorority. I was already more interested in becoming a member of Delta Sigma Theta Sorority, Inc. instead. My mother was a member, which made me a legacy. One of my pageant sisters was a Delta, and she was sweet and humble. I decided, along with my crew, to start pursuing to become a member by attending their events and researching the organization. I later found out that this event affected my younger sister to the point where she wrote a poem about how she felt:

BLACK PEARL

The Black Hills were filled with disparate throngs of people
Awaiting to see the pearls of the Miss Black and Gold Pageant.
But only one pearl stood out
Black, Beautiful and most Brilliant
Exemplifying the struggles and the Beauty of Clams in Her introduction.
Making the snow melt upon the Black Hills as she spoke.
As this Beauty of Black Brilliance rolled away
We heard other introductions,
Boasting and Bragging trying to outshine the Black Pearl,
Trying so eagerly to catch the attention of the sharks.
The introductions ceased and it was time for performance.
Some twinkled their pods,
Others shifted the Hills
But when the Black Pearl strolled out
The Hills were still.
We saw the opening of the Black Pearl's
Mouth as she spoke the words,
"Look at me. Do I appear to be Black, Mahogany, Ebony or
Caramel? Am I Butterscotch, Tan, Yellow? Am I Red or
Can you tell?"
Her performance indeed made the flowers bloom on the
Black Hills.
As the dazzling Pearls lit up the stage for their Q&A session,
Some made the Black Hills stumble; others dampened them.
But when the Black Pearl answered the question of
The qualities she found in her soul mate,
The Yin of the Black Hills rose with applause,
The Yang ever so supported their decision.
So now the moment we've been waiting for,
The crowning of the Black Pearl.
All of the pearls formed a necklace around the stage.
Still none out-shinned the Black Pearl.
The smile of the Black Pearl illuminated an extra light
Across the stage
As two other pearls' names were called for 1st & 2nd runners-up,
Whispers were heard for they knew whose name would be next.
The light of the Black Pearl dropped when an ordinary
Pearl was crowned.
The formation of the Black Hills completely fell,
For it was the light of the Black Pearl that kept
Them standing.

Elizabeth Westbrook, 94'

93

With such a low black population at Texas A&M, I hardly ever saw others that looked like me in class. It was normal for me to be the only one in a class of 200 students. Aside from hanging out in the Commons Area, the way I was able to meet other Blacks was joining certain organizations. I became a member of the Department of the Multi-Cultural Services. The department provided multiple support services for current and prospective students from underrepresented populations and offered diversity education programs that fostered inclusive learning environments for all students. I also got a job on campus as a tutor in Math and Philosophy to student athletes. I was warned to not date any of them, and I listened. I joined the National Association for the Advancement of Colored People (NAACP) for students.

Texas A&M had a Gospel Choir called Voices of Praise. Of course, I joined. I still loved to sing, and I missed being in the choir at church in Houston.

Figure 22: Members of Voices of Praise Gospel Choir in Atlanta, GA at a Convention. Kirsten Westbrook far left

In January of 1995, Voices of Praise had a competition to attend. On a long bus ride from College Station to Atlanta, Georgia, I overheard two male choir members arguing whether women should be allowed to preach or not. They were both Christians from different sects of the religion. They both had strong arguments. Then the strangest thing happened. Both young men pulled out their personal Bibles and turned to scriptures that supported their argument. This blew me away because it clearly showed a contradiction in the Bible and a light bulb went off in my head. Preachers, Pastors, Bishops, and the likes, were all just great storytellers and motivational speakers who use the same book to support whatever message they have. This book that so many live by was completely open to interpretation, and it was solely up to the person in the pulpit what that would be. At that moment, I began to silently question my faith. This was only the beginning.

After my choir sung their set, I went into the balcony to listen to the other choirs and some of the preachers. There was a young man that caught my eye. His eyes were big and chestnut brown. He kept looking at me and started talking to me, and we had a great, intelligent conversation. His name was Bobbie, and I was impressed by him, and when he said he was a preacher, I was really impressed. I thought about how my mother met my father at a convention like this. He told me that he was on schedule to preach, so I stayed to listen to him. I was in awe of this charismatic, well-spoken clever young man. His words mesmerized me, and I was intrigued and wanted to know more. He was there with his father and step-mother, who I met when I met him. When he was done preaching, I expressed how impressed I was and he invited me to eat a late dinner with him and his parents. I gladly agreed. We went to a local diner that

was walking distance away. We talked and talked as we walked. I really liked this guy. Bobbie lived in Dallas and was going to school at Paul Quinn College, but was from Oakland, CA. I wondered how and if we would keep in touch. I felt a connection with him. While at dinner, I revealed that I was a poet, and let them hear a poem. It was the same poem that I performed at the Miss Black and Gold Pageant. It was really the only one I had committed to memory at the time. They loved it, and now he was also impressed with me. The night was lovely, and we had a great time. It was like I knew them already. It did not feel like we just met. It was more like old friends catching up. I liked him and his parents. I wished I had met him sooner because the following day was the last day of the convention.

That next morning, I woke up thinking about my new friend. I decided to write down my information on a sheet of paper just in case he asked for it. I looked for him the whole day and did not see him. Then at the final event of the night, when it was over, I spotted him in the aisle. My heart skipped a beat. I gathered some courage, approached him and greeted him warmly. We made small talk and I waited for Bobbie to ask for my number, but he never did. Disappointed, I began walking away, then I thought, "you only live once." I quickly turned around and handed him the paper with my information on it. The ball was in his court, because I did not get his information. I thought about him all the way back. Two days after returning to campus, Bobbie called.

We talked several times a day. Every conversation was more and more fulfilling. I was delighted with him. He then started sending for me to catch the bus to Dallas on the weekends to spend time with him. I looked forward to it each time. Bobbie lived with his grandparents and his grandmother made the best

blackberry cobbler. She would make some for me every visit. I was surprised that they allowed us to share a room. I felt a little uncomfortable with this because of temptations, but I felt safe because my new boyfriend was a man of God. I trusted Bobbie. The first few visits were great. He always had speaking engagements and attended a Mega Church in Dallas. I loved this church, the pastor and his family. Everyone was so warm and friendly. He introduced me to everyone. I felt so special. Bobbie then started pointing out women in the church that liked him. I didn't like this or understood it. It made me feel uncomfortable and I wondered how he felt about them. I did not see the point in him telling me about every flirt, look, etc. I certainly did not tell him about the young men that were interested in me. Despite how I felt about this, I never questioned him. I did not want to lose him over a petty situation. I thought I was falling in love.

About three months into the relationship, he started bringing up the topic of sex, and I made it clear that I was a virgin and wanted to stay that way until marriage. Bobbie would claim that he was the one that would marry me, so why wait. I was adamant about waiting and he kept trying to convince me. I started to feel that he was a hypocrite. We started fooling around, but I would always stop it if I felt it was going too far. The visits were changing. Bobbie was changing. He started accusing me of cheating all the time and questioned my whereabouts. He began demanding that I give him my entire schedule and explain every place, class I had been in and if I had spoken to any boys. My roommate was very concerned. She could see the stress in my face and hear the fear in my voice when we spoke on the phone. She could not understand why I allowed myself to be treated this way. I just blindly answered Bobbie's questions and tried to be the "good" girlfriend. I found myself spending most of the conversation trying to convince him that I was not cheating on him. Then, he would threaten to break up with me every other week. I would beg him to stay. I could not understand this hold he had on me and thought that it was just love. He had shared some very painful memories from childhood that I helped him deal with, so I attributed this irrational behavior to his childhood traumas. I wanted to save him.

Bobbie's father was an Ex-black panther and Pimp. When Bobbie was younger, his father's prostitutes would touch him. He held on to that pain of his father leaving him alone with those women until I encouraged him to talk to his father about it. He was also physically abused by his mother. Bobbie was the oldest of four and resembled his father. During the times his father was locked up, his mother would beat him for looking like his father, who in turn would beat her whenever he was home. I felt so sorry for his pain and wanted nothing more than to help him or "fix" him. So, when he started treating me poorly, I let him. Bobbie soon escalated from emotional and verbal abuse to physical abuse.

Five months into the relationship, I was spending Memorial Day weekend with Bobbie. The day was fun. He was back to his old self, having a good day. Then later, when we got back home, we started kissing and he laid me down. He was going further than usual, and I asked him to stop. He just kept going. I started squirming and trying to get from under him. He then pulled down my panties, and I kept telling him I did not want to and was not ready. He did not say anything, but he did not stop. I felt a hard thrust and he pushed it in. I said, "No, I don't want to." He finally replied, "Too late, it's in there now." He continued to pound me as he pinned me down. I was in so much pain and could not move. Tears flowed from my eyes, and

I realized nobody would come to my rescue although his grandparents were home. I do not remember if I screamed or not. I felt as if my little spirit just lifted and drifted away. I soon stopped fighting and just lay there. He was not done with me. When he pulled out, he pushed me to the floor on my knees, and put it in my mouth. He held the back of my head and would not let go. He kept going until he was satisfied. I could not breathe and began gagging and choking. As he let me go, I grabbed the small trash can and threw up. He was done with me. I stumbled to the bathroom, blood rolling down my leg. I cleaned myself up. That night, I slept next to him as if nothing had happened. I was terrified and so confused.

I met someone whom I trusted and developed a relationship. Without knowing everything about Bobbie, I trusted myself to be alone with him. He raped and abused me. The Corporate Ego used this Narcissist/ Sociopath to break me, and it worked. This traumatic experience caused me to fear building relationships before knowing as much as I could about someone. I put a wall around myself and did not let people in. The following is a poem I wrote soon after this traumatic experience:

Drifting
I feel paranoid without the fear
My heart is racing with the wind
I can't breathe or speak
I need to scream and yell out
I try, and tears crawl down my face
My thoughts are lost and dark
My father is holding me
I'm only a year old
My mother is now holding him
I watch him drift from her arms
I'm older, in love and afraid
He jams it in and I scream
Virginity is gone; innocence is not
Emotional turmoil takes over

I had been raped but didn't even realize it because it was not what I imagined rape to be. I wasn't attacked by some stranger and I wasn't on a date. I was hanging out with my boyfriend-someone I loved and trusted. I mentally blocked the entire evening out of my mind. Nothing was reported, and I stayed in a relationship with him. He kept doing it. He would take it whenever he wanted it. I would just lay there. I was no match to his wrestling skills that he used to pin me down ensuring I could not fight or get away. Thus, I stopped fighting. I felt trapped and under his spell emotionally. I had lost myself. I was no longer the strong, black woman who was so sure of herself and in control. I was conquered. I stayed with him for eight months.

Whenever I told this story, people would always ask, "Why did you stay?" Why does any woman stay that is a victim of domestic violence? The truth is, I had no idea what had

happened to me. I did not know I was raped. Everything that I read or heard about it did not fit my situation. I was not jumped in some alley by some stranger who beat me up. No one broke in my home and forced themselves on me. It wasn't even date rape because I wasn't on a date. I was with my boyfriend, someone I trusted and thought I loved. Someone I thought I could marry. So, I stayed and forgot about it. My mind blocked it out to protect me, allowing him to do it again and again and again. And I would just lie there, not understanding what was going on.

How did it finally end? The irony is he broke up with me. He called me one night and said he had a confession. He said he lied about never hitting a girl before. He caught his girlfriend before me cheating on him and he followed her home after her date with the other guy. He knew about her date because he looked through her planner. He did the same to me once and confronted me about everything in there. Every male name he asked me about was the name of a building at my school. Bobbie looked through her planner when she wasn't looking, and her date was in there. So, this was premeditated. He pulled up beside them, dragged her out of the car and "beat her like she was a dude." Those were his words. He said he "snapped." Then he went on to say that he did not want to hurt me, so it would be best to go our separate ways. Incongruously, this was the only real act of love he showed me. This was not the first time he wanted to break up with me; he tried several times, but I would always beg him to stay. I didn't beg this time. Something about being beat like a dude didn't sit well with me. He was a boxer and a wrestler. I don't even know if he knew how much damage was already done. I never saw what he did to me as abuse because he never punched me. I kept waiting for that punch. I

used to tell myself, "If he hits me, I'm gone." Well, he pinned me down and forced me to do all sorts of things. But no punching, no throwing me across a room. Just repeated rape, threats, hurtful words, false accusations and mind control. That's what pimps do- control minds. I cried all night because I was confused and did not understand what I was feeling. I later learned that he learned a lot from his father, who was a Pimp and drug dealer. It's a true pimp move, make the victim/abused beg for more pain. In a sense, I was brainwashed. I later discovered that he was cheating on me, which explains why he was always accusing me of cheating.

I was very disturbed by this and believed that I was a "strong Black woman." What I did not realize is that nobody is immune to Narcissists, and they are attracted to certain types of vibrational frequencies. This is how "a strong Black woman" can get caught up. I never thought I would be "that girl"- The one that was abused. Unfortunately, I never reported it, and had nightmares about the abuse for a long time after that. I started to remember. It took me eight years to truly move on. I did this by forgiving. I forgave him, and I forgave myself. He was his father's son, and I was trying to fix him. I learned that I was not the only woman that has tried to fix a man. Never try to "fix" a man. We can only "fix" ourselves. The fact that I endured that pain for eight months meant something was wrong with my self-worth. Could I have really loved myself during that time? Absolutely not.

I am not the only woman who has suffered an abusive relationship unknowingly. We are not taught the tricks of the wolves in sheepskin clothing- especially if our own mothers fell for the same tricks. We are not taught what abuse really is and all the different forms of it. Many women have no idea how

much they would be affected by that. And guess what we do when we get hurt? Nothing. Black women push it to the backs of their minds, get up, go to work and smile. And we think this is being strong- pretending not to be damaged- waiting until we are all alone to cry until our eyes are puffy. We may talk to a "best friend" or a sister about our pain- who usually just empathize and tell you their pain. How does this heal us? It doesn't. We feel better for the moment, but the deep-seated pain remains, because there is really nothing our girlfriends or sisters can do but listen. It takes much more than that.

My lower Chakras were really in trouble, and the more trauma I experienced, the more that came my way. I did not realize how strong I really was to endure repeated rape and survive it without serious mental damage. My spirit was damaged, but not my mind. Like many women, I buried this pain and kept going. The Corporate Ego was not done with me. The goal was to break my spirit. I was already riddled with shame and guilt, but not that much fear. During my Junior year in college, I attracted a stalker, who brought that fear that was missing.

There was a young man obsessed with me that graduated from my school and he began stalking me. He would call me every day, all day long and describe to me what I was wearing and where I had been. He would threaten to have me kidnapped if I was ever alone. He said he had people watching and following me, and when the time came, they would grab me and take me to him. He described in detail how I would be gang raped for their pleasure. I developed a phobia from the fear of the unknown and the fear of being alone. I was paranoid every time I left the dorm. I did not trust any men. I always felt like I was being followed or watched. I was always afraid, and even

tried to report it. As the officer stood in my dorm room witnessing one of the phone conversations, he admitted that he could not do anything because they could not track him, and he was no longer a student. He did tell me that there had been many complaints from other women over the years, but I was the first since he graduated. When he said all the complaints were from women that lived on campus, I knew that was the key to how he was able to watch us and always get our phone numbers. Consequently, I decided to move off campus. Things got better when I pledged and moved off campus. I was never by myself and the stalker could not find me to call me. I don't know if I got over the phobia or if I just found ways to deal with it. That paranoia no longer exists.

In the midst of all of that drama, during the First Semester of my Junior Year, The Nation of Islam lead by Minister Louis Farrakhan, was making a lot of noise in the media and receiving a lot of attention. He called for all able-bodied African American men to come to the nation's capital to address the ills of black communities and call for unity and revitalization of African American communities. On October 16, 1995, more than a million Black men from across the United States gathered together at the National Mall in Washington, D.C. to rally in one of the largest demonstrations in Washington history. This march exceeded the 250,000 who congregated in 1963 for the March on Washington where Dr. Martin Luther King Jr. gave his historic "I Have a Dream" speech. Although the Million Man March was planned and organized primarily by the leader of The Nation of Islam, many religions, institutions, and community organizations across the gamut of Black America joined together, not only for a rally of Black men but also to build what

many saw as a movement directed toward a future rebirth of the Black race.

What did all of this have to do with me, a young college female who was not a part of the Nation of Islam? Well, the Department of Multi-culturalism at Texas A&M presented a writing contest for students to attend an all-expense paid trip to the Million Man March. The Essay had to be on the topic, "What Does It Mean to Be a black Man in America?" I read over the rules of the contest and when I saw that it did not stipulate that only men could participate, I decided to write my essay. I wrote it from the perspective of a Black female. I felt strongly about what this march stood for, being a victim of racism and having witnessed so much. I knew this was an historical event and I wanted to be a part of it.

Several of my friends did not agree that I should enter the contest, arguing what would I know about what it meant to be a Black man. I did not listen to them. Who would know more about being a Black man in this country than a Black woman? Although I thought I would receive discrimination, to my surprise, I was chosen to go on the trip along with seven other students. There was one other female who shared my boldness. Her name was Cedra Brown. I remembered her from the many Delta events I had attended. We were both interested in joining the organization.

Figure 23: Million Man March crowd- A photo taken as I sat on the shoulders of a classmate. This was my view from every angle. A sea of Black faces.

Besides the keynote address by Minister Louis Farrakhan, several prominent speakers addressed those gathered at the Washington Mall including civil rights activists Benjamin Chavis, Jesse Jackson, Rosa Parks, and Dick Gregory. Stevie Wonder entertained the gathering with his songs while Maya Angelou used her poetry to offer advice to the men at the rally. The message of most of the speeches called for black men to "bring the spirit of God back into your lives." These marchers were also encouraged to register to vote to build black political power.

Figure 24: The seven students chosen from Texas A&M to attend the Million Man March with our chaperone on the far right.

March participants took a public pledge to support their families, refrain from violence and physical or verbal abuse toward women and children, and renounce violence against other men "except in self-defense." They also pledged abstinence from drugs or alcohol and to concentrate their efforts on building black businesses and social and cultural institutions in the communities where they lived. The march participants were then asked to "go back home" to implement the changes they had pledged.

This turned out to be one of the most important events of my life. I had a tremendous time. My brother attended the March also, but I only ran into him once. I later learned that Bobbie was there too. My brother stood just a few feet away from him. By this time, my family knew what Bobbie had done to me, and it took every ounce of peace in my brother's body not to retaliate.

This was a March for Peace, and John had to maintain discipline not to confront Bobbie.

Writing and speaking were two things I was confident about and I am so glad I was able to be a part of such an event. As I stood amid all those brothers, I could feel a powerful energy of hope. All the speeches were powerful and heart-felt. I was inspired to write a poem called "Black Hills." When we returned to campus, an event was created to address the topics discussed at the Million Man March. I was on the panel, where I was asked to recite my poem. All of this continued to add strength to my Throat Chakra. Now, I was not only known on my campus, but also surrounding schools that came to participate.

Soon after our return, there was an interest meeting coming up for Delta Sigma Theta Sorority, Inc. Cedra and I had been waiting for this moment for two years. Many of the girls had graduated and the Sorority needed to have a line to keep the sorority alive. This chapter was the Omicron Omega chapter. To have this line, they were assisted by the Brazos County Deltas. I attended the interest meeting and took notes on what I had to do. We had to fill out a detailed application, have proof of a GPA of at least 2.5 with an original transcript. We also had to have three letters of recommendation. One of these letters had to be from a current active Delta. I reached out to my mother to ask one of her friends for this one. We also had to write an essay. All these items were due by a certain date.

Meeting all the requirements and deadlines were intense. I had to depend on people in Houston to write and mail out the recommendations in time. My grades were not as good as high school, and I was cutting it close. I took a class the summer before in Economics. By now, I had changed my major to Accounting/Finance. I changed my mind about becoming an

attorney. I just wanted to graduate. Well, I did well in that class until the final. Some stuff was going on at home and I was totally out of it when I took that test. I bombed it, and it dropped my grade from a B to a D. This really affected my GPA, causing it to be lower than 2.5. I had to have a grade change to meet those requirements. I went to my professor and pointed out how well I was performing before the last test. He looked over my records and agreed to allow me to write a paper to change my grade. I wrote the paper, turned it in and he changed my grade. However, it took time for it to register and show up on the transcripts.

I had everything I needed to turn in except a current transcript. It was the last day to get my packet turned in and mailed off and I still did not have that transcript. I went to have it printed out that morning and the computers shut down. I was freaking out and in full panic mode. They were down for hours. I kept coming back. Around 4:30 pm, the computers came back on. The post office closed at 5:00 pm. It was a line of items that had to go through before mine. I was sweating bullets. At 4:45, my transcript printed out with my current GPA that met the requirements. I quickly sealed my packet and ran as fast as I could to the post office. I got there panting at 4:59 pm. They were closing. When she saw the desperation in my face, she smiled and took the packet. I wanted to faint right there. I could not believe how close that was. If I had not gotten my paperwork turned in, I would not have been considered for the pledging process. This was only the first step. I still had to do an interview.

After about two weeks, I received a letter stating that my application had been accepted. I was confident that I would do fine in the interview, and I did. The final step was for the Deltas to submit all the paperwork to nationals with a list of the

candidates they wanted to continue. Then, Nationals had to respond either accepting, denying or adding to the list. After waiting patiently for my letter of acceptance or denial, I finally received notification that I could continue and would be on the Fall 1995 line. It was thirty of us. We were the Kappa Line and our Line name was "30 Degrees of Eminent Knowledge." We received this name due to the level of intelligence we had on our line. I still keep in touch with my line sisters and they all have lived up to that name. The pledge process was time consuming, stressful, mentally and physically draining; but I would not change a thing. I learned so much about sisterhood and am very appreciative of the hard lessons. These women are some of the most dynamic women I still know. I have always been very proud of this accomplishment.

Figure 25: 30 Degrees of Eminent Knowledge- After the completion of our Induction Ceremony to become members of Delta Sigma Theta Sorority, Inc.

I continued to use my voice to empower myself and others. I became known as a poet and would often be asked to perform or recite poetry on behalf of my sorority or at different events. I had no fear when I would get on stage or in front of a group of people. I was in my element. What never occurred to me was that I should have been studying something along the lines of writing or public speaking. However, my major was Finance and that is what I finally got my degree in. I chose Finance because I thought it would make it easier to get a job after I graduated. I had no intentions to go to graduate school right away. I was tired of school and was eager to work.

My last two years of school, most of my course work was in my major. My classes were much smaller, more like 25 versus 200 like my early years. It was coming to that time to finally graduate. After 4.5 years, I had met all the requirements to receive my undergraduate Bachelor of Arts degree in Finance. The Office of the Registrar is responsible for ensuring the number of graduates at each commencement ceremony results in ceremonies of reasonably equal duration. A total graduating class could easily be over 10,000 students, so the graduations are broken up into Schools of Study. A few weeks before graduation, Mr. Carreathers of the Multi-Cultural Department called me into his office. He was responsible for selecting a student to give the Invocation and Benediction at the graduation. He asked me if I would do it. I was graduating with hundreds of students, and he asked me. I quickly said that I would be honored. But I was curious to why he chose me, so I asked. He said that he respected all the work I had done with speaking at various events and that he knew who my father was. He thought I would be perfect for the job.

August 1997, it was that time. Our graduation was televised and my grandmother was there, along with my mother and siblings. I was the only student to sit on stage. It was a high honor, and I was proud of myself. I was instructed to give prayers that would not offend anyone. I wrote them both out but

attempted to memorize them. I started the ceremonies with the Invocation. I asked everyone to bow their heads and I began to say my prayer. Then I stopped. My mind went blank and I had to reach into my pocket to finish the prayer by reading. The embarrassment I felt had my skin turn a bright red. That pride quickly diminished along with my confidence. When it was time to do the Benediction at the end, I just read straight from the paper, but my voice was still shaky. Everybody was proud of me anyway except my grandmother. She scolded me for messing up. Unfortunately, all the praise I received fell on deaf ears. I only remember messing up on a televised graduation. My grandmother did not have anything nice to say at all. This honor was tainted with words of disempowerment.

Figure 26: August 1997 Graduation at Texas A&M University-Kirsten Westbrook receiving her diploma

Part III: Conscious Being

One may argue how clearing and balancing your chakras can really help a person heal due to it being dealt completely with the spirit and not the physical part of the body. A Conscious Being can deal past the five senses, making dealing with their life trauma very different from others. Their trauma can very easily include matters beyond this realm and, the Corporate Ego uses Narcissistic people to target them to keep them from discovering their life purpose, keeping their chakra system blocked. Helping them to open up to their spiritual gifts using Psycho-energetic counseling will give them the tools they need to discover who they are.

Holistic health and complementary medicine have gotten more attention over the past few decades. People have become interested in studying how the body functions and how energy flows through it, helping them discover their energy system called chakras. "The yogis have used the chakra system for thousands of years as an integral part of holistic healing; knowing that a person's illness often first manifests itself in the chakras, before the body, mind, and emotions. Moreover, they knew that no one could be completely healed if the chakra system continued to be out of balance" (Simpson, 2013, pg. 7).

Once a Conscious Being rids themselves of narcissistic individuals and learns to hone their spiritual gifts through the clearing and balancing of the chakra system, they will be able to discover their purpose for being here by listening within. Later in my adult life, I grew from being a Sentient Being to become a Conscious Being. The trauma I experienced during childhood and in college made me question everything that I had been taught. These questions and that doubt led me to consciousness. My pain eventually led me to my truth.

Black Nationalist Organization

I had already been through so many traumatic events, and I was not even a young adult yet. Being raped and abused by a preacher and realizing what I discovered about being able to use the same Bible to argue two different points, my faith was shot. I did not know what to believe, but I felt religion was full of corruption and unanswered questions. During my Senior year in college in 1997, I started spending more weekends at home. There was a coffee café called Mahogany Café that had opened up where my brother hosted, and my sister performed regularly.

Figure 27: Inside Mahogany Café listening to poetry

(Far left) My sister, Elizabeth Westbrook (Known then as 'Amira'); Kirsten Westbrook; and far right, my sister, Elicia Westbrook

I would go to support them and do some poetry myself. My brother started going to these classes on Sundays at this bookstore near the cafe'. He asked me to come with him to check it out. I was blown away. The elderly gentleman broke down so many things in the Bible and answered several of those questions I kept hidden in my mind. He gave me a book called, "Paul, Disciple or Deceiver." It was a small scroll. I read it very quickly and it pointed out things that I had never thought of that made perfect sense. This was the beginning to a huge chapter in my life. The quote from a <u>Tale of Two Cities</u>, comes to mind: "It was the best of times, it was the worst of times."

My Vibrational Frequency had moved from Negative Three to a positive Two (+2): Awakened. I was no longer "Insecure." This is the beginning of being "Conscious." These are the people who chose the red pill in the popular movie, *The Matrix*. This is when you start to realize that almost everything you have been taught or told was a lie. Ausar Neteru describes this person as someone who has recently connected with their race or national origin and have discovered the farce of religion and the hidden agenda of politics (Neteru 2016, pg. 54-55). The irony is that many that become Awakened fall prey to a Narcissist by way of offering more information. When dealing with Nationalist Organizations, I feel it is very easy to fall from being "Awake" to a Negative One (-1), which is the Slave.

The Narcissist gains control over the newly Awakened by simply showing them a WOW factor that they haven't discovered yet. Thirsty to be the braggart of the Pseudo-revolutionary, Pseudo-political, Pseudo-Enlightened, Pseudo-higher learning circus, the newly Awakened rush to the feet of the Narcissistic religious, political, or nationalist leader to pay homage to yet another walking

encyclopedia of useless information. (Neteru 2016, pg. 55)

I believe I started out "Awakened" when I became a member of this Black Nationalist Organization; but later as I got closer to the founder and leader, I drifted to being a "slave", a vibrational frequency of Negative One (-1), described as the greatest tool of the Narcissist. A slave is typically a person that is the legal property of another and is forced to obey them. In this case, the Slave Master is the Narcissist, but this slave is not forced. The mentality of these people is so broken, that they allow themselves to be used and abused. A person with a slave mentality is one of feeling inferior or of feeling lost without hope, a feeling that they do not have the power to significantly alter their own circumstances. A person conditioned to quietly, and without objection, accept harmful circumstances for themselves as the natural order of things. They're also conditioned to accept their master's view and beliefs about themselves, and strive to get others, within their group, to accept the master's view. "The Narcissist does not have to get the slave to accept abuse because they believe they deserve it because they have accepted an existence of being less and therefore feel worthless." (Neteru 2106, pg. 54). Members of nationalist groups and cults that blindly follow a leader, without questions, are examples of modern-day slaves. I was one of these people.

"I came giving you what you want so you that you may learn to want what I have to give." These are the infamous reiterated words of that leader and establisher of the Afrikan-Spiritual Science- a way of life that many thought to be incumbently necessary for the spiritual development and re-education of African-Americans in the West. This leader created

a System of tools based upon the ancient Ha Kha teachings of the Supreme Grand Hierophant Tehuti. He introduced his teachings first in 1963, during a time when Black America was in total chaos and in a lot of pain. He continued teaching until early millennia when he was arrested and convicted and sentenced to life in prison. He was the author of the book that intrigued me so, and hundreds of other books covering every religious belief, black nationalist organizations and life beyond this planet. The titles of each scroll were carefully chosen to catch the eye of any curious soul, and it worked.

He saw a need and created a philosophy to fill that need. African Americans in the West wanted religion, but really did not know which religion they wanted, or which was best. Most of us did not even understand what the word "religion" meant. All we knew of religion were Christianity and Islam. We had been cut off from the 'old time religion', but deep down in our very souls we were crying, freedom, justice, equality- again with our limited definitions of what these principles really meant. We had a wrenching gut feeling, a severe hunger; we were yearning to be 'tied back' to that place where it all began so our souls could be fed directly from its source. Some called that place "Africa", some said "The Motherland," not realizing that the entire Earth is the Motherland of the entire Black Nation. Nature gave us solutions that were practical and applicable for the time periods of our calling. She gave us lessons that were conducive to our three-dimensional environment and political stance. During the 1920s, in the disguise of the doctrine of Marcus Garvey, many heard the call for rapture; perhaps the brave-hearted amongst the wretched. But that was only the beginning. As powerful as Garvey was, and as astonishing as his empire was, it was only preparation for the ultimate lessons of cultural-

empowerment that was to come. However, at the time White America was flabbergasted by the rise of this Nation, with the huge strapping black men dressed in pinstriped suits and bow ties, riding on horseback throughout the streets of Harlem New York, with the propagation of "the Journey Home to Africa." Garvey left us a signature, a declaration that it can be done; a confirmation that we can aspire and achieve great things if we can only unite under some basic principles.

Then, we had the coming of the "Messenger," as those who believed called the Honorable Elijah Muhammad, founder and leader of the "Black Muslims" in America known as The Nation of Islam. He presented the concept of taking responsibility as gods of the earth and the universe- 'do for self' was the motto. This created much tension within the hierarchy system of America and her allies. They could not allow a time bomb to exist with the house; it had to either be stopped or be controlled by them. Muhammad consequently spoke of the 'lamb'- the one that would lead this black Nation toward the final path. The leader I am referring to but shall remain nameless claimed to be this 'lamb'. He presented what he called the true religion of the Black man and woman under a fourth-dimensional applied science of sound right reasoning. He used these teachings to make Black Americans feel they were being "tied back" to the place where it all began.

I was not only a member of this organization, I had a personal relationship with him, one that proved to be very toxic. I was a loyal student and felt as if this leader filled that void in my life from losing my father. I respected him and loved him for the greatness I saw in his brilliance. However, he taught and ran his organization with intimidation and fear. He played mind

games with people, especially women. I dropped everything in Houston and moved to be closer to this organization.

I had a degree in Finance, and it did not take long to find a job in the small town at a local bank. Little did I know, the local townspeople did not like the members of this Black Nationalist Organization that took refuge in the adjacent town. It was unheard of for Blacks to own so much land. The members of this organization did not only stand out because they were Black, but they dressed differently and wore their hair a certain way. I had to endure daily slander of the organization and be very careful. Only two months after working there, some fellow members spotted me in the bank and gave greetings. My supervisors witnessed this interaction and two days later, I was fired. I immediately called the office of the organization to seek help. During my spare time and on the weekends, I would go up to the land and volunteer. Every Saturday night, there was class with the leader, who would teach on various subjects.

The land was open to the public during the day and on Saturday nights. I was in awe of the property that was adorned with Egyptian statues. It was beautiful. When I would go up there, I would be greeted at the gate and had to state my business. So, although it was open, it was guarded. I was considered a "runner." Many of the people that lived on the property could not drive, so volunteers who had cars would run errands for the land. I would take people shopping, make bank runs, etc. When I lost my job, I was volunteering every day and one day, one of the elder women asked to speak to me when I returned from making a run. It was a Friday, September 4, 1998.

"Greetings" greeted an older short statured woman. I knew she was someone important and I was very curious what she wanted to talk about. "I understand that you lost your job at the bank?"

"Yes mam. They found out I was associated to our organization and fired me. I was still in my probationary period, so they did not have to give me a reason why," I answered.

"I've been looking over your application and we could use someone with your skills here on the land. Would you be willing to live here and work with us?" She was smiling slightly as she dropped a huge bomb in my lap. I had spoken to and met so many people that dreamed of living on the property, and even more that tried, asked and was turned down. I was in slight shock.

Stammering, I responded, "Of course, I mean yes. I would be honored." I felt so special and privileged to be asked. Without giving it any thought, I agreed. I moved up the very next day, Saturday, September 5, 1998.

I did not know what I was getting into and was too naïve to think it through. When you move on the land, you are assigned to a division or given a job. This is a non-paying job. However, everything is provided for you. You get food, shelter and the basic needs. When you need toiletries, you must submit a request to the Finance Department. This was the department that I was supposed to work in because of my degree. However, when I was mated, my job changed to the Census Department. Nevertheless, I was excited to be there and was willing to help in any area that I could.

The first few weeks were pretty much the same and I hardly ever saw the leader. Then one day he sent a message for all the sisters in the office to come to the studio. He had a teenage

son that was recording an album. There was a music side to the leader. He was a singer and music producer. He needed female voices to record a phrase.

This was my first time in the studio, and I was amazed. As he was giving instructions to the ladies on what he wanted them to do and the energy level they needed, he mentioned that he was in a fraternity. It just so happened to be the brother fraternity to my sorority. So, I boldly told him. He just nodded, and then asked where I was from. He noticed I had a Southern accent and made fun of it. I was happy for the interaction and was elated that I had a connection to the leader. I had so much fun in the studio. It was a nice break from my job in Census which was mainly secretarial duties. This was my first good day.

One day I got sick and could not go into work. It just so happened this was one of the days that the leader came to the office. He very seldom walked through there, and you could go days without seeing him up close. When he noticed that I was not there he asked about me. The ladies told him that I was sick and was at home in bed. I suffered from asthma, but I did not have asthma when I lived in Texas. I developed it when I moved here. During the summer months, my asthma was bad, and I suffered an asthma attack and had to stay home.

The leader got on his walkie-talkie and told my mate to get me some medicine and to check on me. He then informed one of the sisters to check on me as well. He made a big deal about making sure I got better. He also had a message for me. He wanted to start a newspaper and he wanted me to be one of the writers.

One of the sisters came running to me with a walkie-talkie screaming, "The leader wants to talk to you!" I jumped up and answered on the walkie-talkie.

"How are you doing? Did you receive your medicine?" he asked.

"I'm doing much better now that I've heard your voice. No, I didn't get any medicine." I replied, grinning from ear to ear, still in shock. As I lay in bed sick, I had no idea that I was being discussed on the radio, so when the sister came running in the room, I did not know what was going on. He then proceeded to find out who was supposed to bring me the medicine and why they had not brought it yet. He informed the sister and told her to hurry and bring me the medicine. This was all on the radio for all to hear. I was so surprised because the leader very seldom spoke to anyone on the walkie-talkie but the brothers. I had no idea that he even remembered who I was and was so happy to have a different job that would challenge me.

I was working on the newspaper with one other sister. However, I was the chief editor and did most of the work and would stay late to meet deadlines and finish.

I had to write articles, find pictures and lay out the newspaper. Once all articles were finished, I would lay out the paper on 11 x 17 sheets to show how it would really look once printed. Then I would turn it in to the leader to look over it and proofread it. Then I would get the paper back covered in red ink with corrections, additions and things to take out. Before the newspaper was ready, he decided to get us a printer that would print 11 x 17 paper just for our Department. He gave us money to get the printer, and we had a runner take us to pick it up.

I continued to work on the newspaper and layout of the paper to get it ready. I was very good at being able to implement every correction the leader made, no matter what, and still making everything fit. He was impressed by my work ethic and ability to follow instructions.

Soon the first newspaper was ready for print. I had to find a printing company in an adjacent town and develop a business relationship with this printing company for all the future newspapers. When the newspaper finally was ready for pickup, it came out very good. The leader was very pleased and passed out newspapers to as many people as he could. The newspaper idea came because the Publication Department was writing flyers. The organization was having a lot of trouble with the townspeople and being targeted. This was a small town whose population was predominantly Caucasian people. They did not like that an African male owned the largest amount of land in the entire town. They also did not like that he was building and had businesses on his property. They were coming onto the property almost daily to see what he was doing. So aside from the books, The Publication Department started fighting by printing flyers telling our side of the story and pointing out the corruption that was taking place in town. I helped with these flyers and this is how the leader discovered I could write. I had made my mark and a name for myself on the land. I was the newspaper lady. Many of the other sisters started to respect me when they realized I was not going anywhere and that my skills were much needed.

After working on the newspaper for a while, the leader came to me and told me about a job in a nearby town working for a local newspaper. There was a lady in the organization that knew they had a job opening because she was working there. He wanted me to learn all about the business of newspapers to help

better the newspaper that we had. Also, many of the local newspapers would print very one-side articles about the organization that were slanderous and negative. Usually, we would respond with a flyer, but if I could actually work for a newspaper, I would have more pull to try and promote a positive side. He told me to go interview for the job and try to get it. I felt honored to do this and I went and got the job as a writer for this local newspaper.

At first my duties were to write certain articles, proofread articles and do minimal office tasks. When the publisher of the newspaper saw how good I was at everything I did, he started to give me more responsibility. I started doing Graphics and Design and creating advertisements for local businesses. I also helped with the layout of the newspaper. He even sent me to school to learn web design. I really liked the freedom of working and felt normal again.

The publisher of the newspaper tried to understand the organization and was very supportive when it was time to print positive articles about the organization. But he could clearly see that I was being controlled. He told me that they were ready to just discharge me the first minute I got in trouble and because of this, he would give me even more responsibility and tried to make sure I had opportunities to move up. He asked me to host his talk show that was on a local TV station. It was a show highlighting things going on in the local community and adjacent towns. I was very happy about this and loved the fact that I would be on television and have the opportunity to interview all types of people. I was promoted to Editor of the newspaper and decided to put forth my energy in my job and move up politically in the city.

Figure 28: Local Bishop in Macon, GA being interviewed by Kirsten Westbrook for TV show

There was a position opening on a political panel that I was going to try to go for. I would have to be voted on to this panel for it to work. The publisher was trying to help me make a name for myself so that I would receive these votes. I was making a name for myself and gaining respect from local officials. His plan was working, and I was being considered for the political position on the panel. This would have given me power to make decisions for the city.

After working at the newspaper for over a year I had developed a strong relationship with the publisher like daughter/father. I was even close to his family. It was the Summer of 2001, and the leader told anybody who worked outside the land to quit their jobs.

I really did not want to quit because I was about to be named to this political panel and I loved being a talk show host. But I informed the publisher that I could no longer work there, and I finally quit my job. This was yet another traumatic experience and the feeling of losing a father all over again.

My actions were those of a "slave" on the True Number Line. As much as I wanted to improve my own life, I chose to do what I thought the leader wanted me to do, just to be on his "good side."

Things were pretty normal until one day in Spring 2002, the leader was going out. While he was out, the land was raided by the Federal Bureau of Investigations (FBI) and other law enforcement.

I was working on the computer when I heard loud noises and a police officer asking for everyone upstairs to come down. All the sisters were very frightened and none of them were moving, so I got up. As I went to the top of the stairs, there was a man there halfway up the stairs pointing a gun at me. I immediately put my arms up because I was afraid. He started yelling at me and then came up the stairs still pointing the gun at me. He motioned for everyone to gather to one side of the room. My fear caused me to start to hyperventilate. I was having an asthma attack. One of the sisters had to inform the officer what was going on and asked if she could get my inhaler out of my purse. The officer allowed the sister to get the inhaler and after a few puffs, I was fine. We were all told to go outside and stand under the Pavilion. We had no idea what was going on but had a feeling it had something to do with all the trouble we had been having in town with zoning laws and issues. The local authorities had come to the land several times to do searches and such but never found anything. It was just pure harassment.

Several months after the raid, law enforcement ceased the land and we had 7 days to move off the property. This whole

experience affected my root chakra due to the fear of being held at gunpoint and losing my home. The root chakra is all about survival and feeling secure. This moved me to negative three on the True Number line, which is "insecure" because I no longer felt protected. This mental state was a catalyst for future decisions I made.

Chapter 9

Marriage & Relationships

The next chapter in my life was about to begin. The first time I saw Terry, he walked in the studio where the choir rehearsing. It was September 2003. His polo style shirt was neatly tucked in and buttoned up to the top and his head was shaved completely bald. My eyes followed him in amazement as he walked toward our director to introduce himself. He was there to help the choir. I was very impressed by his voice and his skill in teaching the choir the acapella songs. He was the son of one of the choir members who grew up singing with the Church of Christ, a religion that does not use instruments. They use their voices to create music. Terry had an expert ear.

The Leader told me that he had a vision about my future husband. He described him as being a good Christian man that was not gay and that we would have son. I thought this was a peculiar description. He also mentioned that it was someone that he had never met. He said he did not recognize him. He mentioned this vision to me a few times, each time adding little details.

When I met Terry, I truly believed this was the man in the prophecy. One day during choir rehearsal while Terry was working with the alto section that I was in, he got eye contact with me and then jumped and immediately left the circle. Everybody in the circle was surprised and did not know why Terry suddenly left, but it was right when he got eye contact with me. This was the first time that our eyes had locked. Before

now, we would just glance at each other in passing but never locked eyes. That evening was the first time he decided to have a conversation with me and get to know me. I finally asked him why he left the group when he locked eyes with me. Terry would not explain at first, but later told me that he saw the same aura or light image around me that he had seen in a dream that he had about his soulmate. After rehearsals, he began talking to me and we developed a friendship. He initially only came to help us, but soon he decided to join the choir.

Because he fit the description of the prophecy and him dreaming about me, I was convinced that this was the man that was supposed to be my husband. When we had performances or a parade to attend outside the land, I would ride with him and his family. This was my only opportunity to spend some time with him. I liked him very much and he liked me as well. Soon, he started picking me up to spend weekends with him. We both knew that the brothers on the land would not like this, but we did not care. The brothers gave Terry a hard time, because many of them had shown interest in me, but I did not return the interest. Subsequently, when brothers would approach me, and I knew that the Leader knew them, I would immediately turn them down. The Leader said he did not know the man in his vision, so I knew these guys were not it. I never even asked or thought about if this man would be a good husband, I just desired to meet the man in the vision. I just wanted to fulfill the prophecy. As you see, I was still a "slave", willing to base my entire future relationship on a vision.

After getting to know Terry for about six months later in March, Terry proposed to me. Terry called my mother to ask permission and get her blessing. My mother was very happy for

129

me and was very supportive. A few months after being engaged, I got pregnant. This was a planned pregnancy because I suffered from polyps in my uterus. My doctor told me that getting pregnant would help stop the polyps from forming. Polyps are a growth in the uterus that causes the uterine wall to shed and bleed. They are caused by high levels of stress. During January, I bled the entire 3 weeks. Thus, once I was engaged and knew that I was going to marry Terry, I did not mind getting pregnant to stop the polyps from growing back. I did not take into consideration that I had not known Terry very long; I had only met him the September before. I got pregnant in the summer and we got married August 9, 2004.

When I was about five months pregnant, I got a call from my mother saying that my grandmother did not have long. It was recently discovered that she had cancer and she hid it from us for years. My mom asked that we come see her before it's too late. My older sister and I got plane tickets to get there as quick as possible. It was supposed to be a quick trip to visit my grandmother. After my mother told my grandmother that we were coming, she transitioned. She passed away while we were in the air. I was devastated and riddled with guilt and disappointment. I wanted my grandmother to meet my baby. She had removed us from her will when we joined the organization, and our relationship was never the same. I always felt a connection to her and loved her dearly. She was stern and strong, and I admired her. Not getting a chance to say goodbye to my grandmother affected my energy system and was also traumatic.

When Elicia and I got to Houston, we helped my mother plan the funeral. Terry rented a car and was going to drive down. The funeral was an opportunity for everyone in the family to

meet my husband. My grandmother's favorite song was Amazing Grace, so my sister, Terry and I decided to sing it at the funeral. I choked up and messed up my part- more guilt. I could feel my grandmother's disappointment. The familiar feeling of when I stumbled over my prayer at my college graduation was present. Many of the people at the funeral did not let me forget my mess up. They kept pointing out how could I forget the lyrics to "Amazing Grace." I felt so disempowered. I don't know what happened up there. I guess it was a trigger. Performing in front of my grandmother, whether she was in this dimension or the next, was a struggle for me. It triggered a childhood memory of vacation bible school at my grandmother's church in Waco, TX. I was asked to pray in front of everyone for a program, and my grandmother wrote it for me to memorize. I froze and had to read the prayer. It dawned on me that she was the reason I failed at my college graduation. I had a desire to please her, but I never could- not even at her funeral. This put me back at negative three on the number line, insecure. I was also suffering from approval addiction.

> I was amused after discovering that the illusion of love painted on the canvas of human ignorance was nothing more than another form of approval addiction in which people forced themselves into something they thought was necessitated to feel valued. They thought that another's caring for them might give them personal validity. (Neteru, 2016, pg. 21)

The above quote is referencing the illusion on being "in love" and how people rely on others to feel validated. I needed to feel valued. I needed to redeem myself for messing up my prayers. I needed to feel that my grandmother was proud of me.

This "approval addiction" was also the reason why I accepted so much in my marriage. I wanted my friends, family and co-workers to look at my family and my husband and think, "good job."

Seeing my family after so many years was nice. They all seemed to like my husband. And funny enough, he looked almost identical to my first cousin, Jamail- my mother's brother's son. After the funeral, I rode back to Georgia with my husband. There was a surprise waiting for me when I got home. Before I left, I had been sleeping on an air mattress, which caused me to have back pain and many sleepless nights. While I was gone, Terry got us an entire bedroom set. A real bed! I was excited and extremely grateful.

Although we were in a good place and hardly ever argued, the truth was that I really did not know him at all. I only knew what he wanted me to know. I married him before knowing him for a full year and was about to have his baby. My doctor was a friend of the family. My son's due date was March 8, 2005. My entire pregnancy, I prepared my body for a healthy natural birth. Friday, February 25th, I went in for my checkup and my doctor said that the baby's heart rate was rapid, and he wanted me to check myself into the hospital that night. He explained that he would not be on call the day the baby was due, and he wanted to be the one to deliver my baby. He said he would check on me when he came in and if there were no changes, he would have to induce. We did as he suggested. After checking myself in, the OBGYN on call came to check on me. She said that I was perfectly fine and that she would send me home, but it was up to my doctor. My doctor finally came early Saturday morning. When he came in, he asked, "Did they induce

yet?" He never even checked me. The nurses said no, and he ordered them to start inducing. Inducing labor is the artificial start of the birth process through medical interventions or other methods. Induction not done for medical reasons or as an emergency is considered elective, but I did not elect this. I was tired and confused and wanted to speak up, but I didn't. I trusted him. It was not working. I was only dilating about a centimeter every three hours. I needed to be about 10 centimeters for the baby to be born. I could not walk around or do anything to help my baby drop. After about 12 hours, I asked for the epidural. These induced contractions were extremely painful. Finally, early Sunday morning, after being in labor for about 26 hours, he suggested a caesarian. They had already broken my water and I was 8 centimeters. I reluctantly agreed. I was ready for this baby to come out and I was too weak and numb to push. They would have had to pull my baby out with forceps. My son was born Sunday, February 27, 2005. I had a boy just like the Leader said I would.

In May of 2006, I found out I was pregnant. This pregnancy was not planned but I was excited. After announcing it to some friends, I went to the bathroom and noticed blood. I passed a huge blood clot and felt very week. I took myself and my son to the emergency room. I called my sister to come get my son while I saw the doctor. Although my blood showed that I was still pregnant, my hCG levels were too low. hCG is the hormone called human chorionic gonadotropin that is produced during pregnancy. It is made by cells formed in the placenta, which nourishes the egg after it has been fertilized and becomes attached to the uterine wall. Levels can first be detected by a blood test about **11 days after conception** and about **12-14**

days after conception by a urine test. Usually, the hCG levels will double every 72 hours. The level will reach its peak in the first **8-11 weeks of pregnancy** and then will decline and level off for the remainder of the pregnancy. I was about 6 weeks pregnant, so my levels should have been high, but they were low as if I were only about two weeks instead of six.

The doctor said I was having a "spontaneous abortion", also known as a miscarriage. I looked at him confused and started asking questions. He explained that my body was passing the fetus and it happens with about 20% of pregnancies. He said there is no known cause and it was not my fault. He then said that it would be best to get the rest of the fetus out by performing a Dilation and curettage (D&C), which is a brief surgical procedure in which the cervix is dilated and a special instrument is used to scrape the uterine lining. He said it would help prevent infections and heavy bleeding. I was devastated and broke down right there in the hospital. This was traumatic and affected my sacral chakra. Although Terry was supportive, I felt alone in my pain. I put this in the back of my mind and never spoke of it.

About a month later, Terry and I decided to move back to Texas to be closer to family. He has two daughters from his first marriage that he had not seen in many years. I moved first so he could finish out his contract. The plan was to move into a house my grandmother owned and that my mother grew up in, but it needed a lot of work. The house was not ready, so I moved in with my mother. I decided to get my teacher certificate since I had a degree. I went through Texas Teachers that summer and was able to get hired by the time school started. When Terry got to Texas, he struggled finding work due to some trouble from

his past. So, he started his own business fixing and selling computers, doing websites, and other things technical.

Towards the end of 2006, I got pregnant again. I explained to Terry that we needed more income into the household, so Terry began doing contract work that helped a little. With this pregnancy, I decided to do a home birth with a mid-wife. When she got my medical records from my first birth to see why I had a cesarean, she told me I was robbed of a natural birth. She said I was one centimeter from crowning and that my cesarean was completely unnecessary. I felt like I was tricked. The recovery from that was six weeks. I could hardly walk after and could not hold my baby for weeks. The good news was that I did not have any major medical issues and I was cleared to have a home birth. My second son was born August 22, 2007.

During the Christmas holiday that year, we went to Dallas. Terry decided to try and see his daughters, so we went to their church. Every number we had for them was changed or disconnected. They were having a revival during that week, but his ex-wife and daughters were not there. But they were still members, so Terry left a note and pictures for his daughters and their mother at the church. We never heard from them and did not know if they even got the note and pictures. Then, a few months later, the Attorney General served Terry with papers to go to court for child support. He blamed his ex-wife and was very upset. He complained that she used the information we gave her to turn him in instead of allowing him to communicate with his daughters. As the court dates kept coming, I decided to call one of my line sisters who was a family attorney to help. I was now pregnant with my third child.

Ironically, Mary, his first wife, started allowing us to see the girls. I loved them all from the start. The girls were respectful and smart. I thought Mary did an excellent job raising them on her own. She had recently remarried and her new husband along with her youngest convinced her to let the girls meet their father. I developed very close relationships with her and her daughters. Many found this odd that the second wife could be friends with the first wife, but we just simply got along.

Things seemed somewhat normal for now. However, the most tragic event in my life was yet to come. On January 7, 2009, I gave birth to a healthy baby boy. This was my third child and was not planned. I had just lost about 15 pounds doing a weight loss challenge at work when I noticed I was late. I left work during lunch to buy a pregnancy test after talking to our nurse. It was positive. Instead of being happy, I was worried. My husband was still unemployed, and we were living check to check. My second son was only a year old. After a rough second year teaching, I decided to change schools. My husband had a lead to get a job near Katy, a suburb Northwest of Houston, so I interviewed with schools in that area. I got a job at Watkins Middle School, but my husband did not get the job. I commuted for over an hour to work for a while, then we moved to that area.

Watkins was great and low stress compared to my previous school. I found a great daycare for the boys right around the corner from the school. I used the same midwife for this pregnancy that I used for my second son. I was having trouble making payments. She did not take insurance and I had to pay out of pocket. One night, I had a nightmare that my child was born not breathing. I woke up crying and sweating. I could hardly breathe. I called my mother and told her the dream. She

calmed me down and advised me not to repeat the dream or tell anyone else. I listened. On January 6th, I woke up and on my way to the bathroom, water started trickling down my leg. It was early. I went to my midwife and she checked me. My water did not break fully, and I was only dilated a few centimeters. My contractions were not consistent, so I knew I was not in labor. She called me that night to check on me and said she would come the following morning to help me go into labor.

We had a projector in our living room, and she advised me to put on something that I really liked to help not think about the pain of the contractions. I put on Beyonce's Birthday concert and videos. I am still a huge fan, and at the time, Halo was my favorite song. I was told to walk back and forth and squat every time I felt a contraction. She would check me every 20 minutes to see if I was dilating. I don't remember how long it took, but the squatting worked. I gave birth to an 8 lb 13 oz baby boy, 21 inches long. One of my line sisters that lived nearby came and recorded it. He had an old soul, looked a little like my oldest and was beautiful. He cried more than my first two and wanted to be held. I didn't want to spoil him, so I would let him cry. But eventually, I would give in and pick him up.

Soon after he was born, my husband had to go to court for child support. Money was tight, and I had to ask my mother to help me pay the balance for my son's delivery. The months following were the hardest of my life.

It was a Monday at the end of February. I had just returned to work the week before. I woke up that morning and nursed my newborn baby. My oldest son had a fever and had to stay home. My husband stayed home with the baby and my

oldest. I gathered my middle son and we left. Our cell phones were cut off due to the bill not being paid, and I had to stay after school for a parent-teacher conference, so I got home later than usual. It was a little after 4:00 when I pulled in my driveway. I was engorged and ready to feed my baby. When I got out the car, a police officer came out of my house and asked me who I was. I could see another officer inside consoling Terry. Terry had my oldest in his arms holding him tightly, screaming, "He stopped breathing! He stopped breathing!"

I informed the officer that I lived there as he motioned to the other officer to close the door. He would not let me in. "Something happened to your baby," he said calmly. He stood with his had held out as if he was blocking me.

"What? What happened? Where is he?"

"He was unconscious. He is at the hospital. The ambulance took him."

"Is he alive?" I asked gripping myself on my van. I was getting light-headed.

"I don't know ma'am," he replied, looking sorry for me.

Suddenly, my neighbor approached with a bottle of water, giving it to me. The officer immediately ordered her to go back. "What hospital?"

"You can follow me, and I will take you there. Is that okay?"

I nodded and got in my van. I prayed all the way to the hospital. I told myself that it was asthma or something that could be easily fixed. I parked and was led into a room. I was told to

sit on a couch. When I sat down, I called Terry and told him I was at the hospital but did not know anything yet. I did not like that we were not allowed to communicate. A doctor came in and sat in a chair in front of me.

"When your son came in, he was unconscious and not breathing. We were never able to revive him. We ran many tests. We called time of death at 4:00. There was no sign of suffocation or choking. We think it may be SIDS, but we are still running tests." The doctor explained.

"What? What did you say?" I thought I misheard him.

"I am so sorry for your loss. These are grief counselors if you need to talk. They are here to help. Do you need us to contact anyone for you?" He was pointing to a lady sitting in a chair to my right and another one who had sat on the couch next to me. I had not noticed them before. There were others all just staring at me with these sad eyes. I was in shock. I just sat there for a moment.

Tears started strolling down my cheeks, "I don't understand. He was fine this morning. I fed him before I went to work. He was not sick. He was fine. I don't understand. I don't understand. Where is my baby? I need to nurse him. Where is my baby?" I was rambling hysterically. I was looking at all of them, waiting for an answer. They said nothing. The one next to me just held me. I was confused and needed answers.

Six weeks and five days after his birth, he went to sleep and did not wake up. My child was gone. After all the tests, it was ruled as Sudden Infant Death Syndrome (SIDS). This was a devastation like none other. When I tried to talk to Terry to get these answers, he would say a little, then shut down. All I know

is that he was doing laundry downstairs after feeding the baby around 10:00 that morning. He said he fell asleep on the couch and when he woke up the house was quiet. He made the baby a bottle and when he checked on him, he was not breathing. Our cell phones were down, but the house phone was on, so he called 911. We were investigated, but no foul play was determined.

My sister has the gift to connect with the other side and was in contact with my son. She said he missed me and wanted me. Knowing that he was okay, kept me from going crazy. That helped me to be strong. We had a small funeral within a few days and my school sent over pot-luck dinners for after. My mother paid for the funeral and my mother in-law prepared the body with a ritual. I was holding up until I saw that small casket. I fell to my knees screaming for my baby. I just wanted to hold him one more time.

After that, I could not bear to be around babies or pregnant women for about two years. It would send me in a spiraling depression. My heart would beat fast, I would shake and just want to cry. My mind and body would react. I became extremely over-protective of the two children I already had. I was always afraid I might lose them too. I did not like going places or being in public. This was the fear of death that led to a phobia that controlled my life. I don't know what changed, but my feelings did a 180 degree turn and I yearned for another child to fill that void. That is how my daughter came to be. She was born September 22, 2011. But when she was born, I watched her like a hawk. I feel time has healed this wound. But I did not want any more kids.

From being in a cult, a troubled marriage, and losing a child, my entire chakra system was blocked. I was totally lost and had married someone who I hardly knew. There were many secrets and lies deep seeded in our marriage that we both struggled with. Trying to fulfill a prophecy and being desperate made me blind to the red flags. I tried to focus on the present and the future and not judge him for his past mistakes. We desperately wanted to fix our marriage and learn to trust each other again. Unfortunately, that trust was never restored, and we divorced January 2016.

Part IV: Ascended Master

How does the gravitational pull of the universe relate to human emotion and energy? Psychologists learn that energy is like gasoline: we fuel up with a healthy diet, sleep and exercise, then we set out to face the world. I will argue that energy does not only come from diet, sleep and exercise, but that we are influenced by a widespread network of energy fields imperceptible to our five senses. An Ascended Master that has fallen victim to their own personal trauma can use the knowledge of energy types and emotional types to ensure they balance their chakra system and do what they returned here to do.

Spirituality, meditation and the fact that I know there is no such thing as death has helped me deal with the death of my son. I had to unlearn my fears just like I learned them. I no longer feared the unknown or death. I am a living example of how a healthy diet, proper sleep and exercise is not enough to have a healthy energy system. There is much more at stake.

> We live in a world of violence, selfishness, an erratic economy, and scary diseases- as well as a world of love, miracles and healing. All this affects our energy, while our own energy affects the people around us. We are part of great swirling invisible energy fields, positive and negative, that shape personal and planetary health. (Orloff, 2004, pg. 4).

Our soul is the voice of our energy and emotional system. Knowing how to fight against negative energy by clearing your chakra system and empowering yourself with the knowledge of

the different Energy and Emotional Types, an Ascended Master can be very powerful.

During childhood, I grew up in a big house and had everything I needed. I never feared poverty from my family growing up. However, once I got married and we struggled financially, the fear of poverty set in. I feared not being able to provide for my children everything that was provided for me. I always had this sense that I knew more than the average person- that I had some inside scoop into things, so I never feared not knowing. I grew up around scholars, doctors, preachers, nurses, teachers, etc. It was like I was blessed genetically to be smart or learn things easily. I have always been attracted to information and wanted to know more, because my family gave me that strong feeling of just knowing.

A personal value system is a set of principles or ideals that guide a person's behavior. Values are general principles to normalize our day-to-day conduct. They not only give direction to our behavior but are also morals and intentions in themselves. Values deal not so much with what is, but with what ought to be; in other words, they express ethical imperatives. They are the expression of the ultimate ends, goals or purposes of social action. Our values are the basis of our judgments about what is desirable, beautiful, proper, correct, important, worthwhile and good as well as what is undesirable, ugly, incorrect, improper and bad. We develop this value system from our family, social network (relationships), education, media, exposure (life experiences) and spirituality.

Chapter 10
Bio-Vibrational Science & The Narcissist

In 2012, my younger sister invited me to the Self-Empowerment Center. Here, they study Bio-Vibrational Science, which is the study and process of managing the energy flow within biological and environmental systems. My brother was the musician there and she said the teachings were phenomenal. I went, and a new journey in my life began. I wanted and needed more. This desire of more knowledge put me at Positive Five on the Scale of Vibrational Frequency, The Seeker. "The Seeker is a person who has firmly decided that there is something more and that they will not be stagnated by tradition or a nagging guilt to stay in the same mindset because everyone else around them is in that mindset" (Neteru, 2016, pg. 66-67). From these teachings and applying them, I began to learn who I was and my purpose. This was the beginning of my healing. "It is through my pain that I teach," said Ausar Neteru, the AcharYah or teacher at the Self-Empowerment Center. These words resonated with me because it is also through my pain that I am able to help others. It is through my survival of past traumas that I can empathize with others. This is where I learned my purpose and how I had to battle my biggest enemy, the Narcissists in my life, to fulfill this purpose.

My first two visits to The Self-Empowerment Center were by myself. When I walked into the dark building, a strong energy filled me up and a wonderful smell invited me in. It was so different from anything that I had ever experienced. On my third visit, I filled out a form to join. I learned through becoming a student of Bio-vibrational Science that I am an Ascended Master. I have always known of some greatness inside of me but struggled finding it and using it to find my true purpose. There is an immenseness inside of me burning to come out! And I want to share it with the world. I want my words to set people free; like Harriet Tubman. My freedom will lead to other people's freedom- changing lives one word at a time. I used to think that freedom of the mind was knowing where you come from. I was wrong. Freedom is knowing where you are going. When I discovered this, I could not stop crying because I was realizing and feeling a little bit of freedom- just a little- Freedom Tears. My life was getting mad at me for not living up to my potential and life started happening. The teachings started a process inside of me. They were starting to free me up. My soul had been crying out for a while and I just wasn't listening. There had been a block of depression that was deep seeded. A man that is willing to fight forever won't have to fight for long. Make your results your revenge.

Being an Ascended Master allowed me to handle my fears in a positive way versus a negative one. From the fear of failure and the fear of death, I pushed myself to accomplish what I set out to do and maintain a healthy lifestyle. But there were still deep-seeded issues that I needed to deal with to live my purpose. It was January 2014, and the AcharYah was giving a lesson on Narcissists. It was this lesson that I realized I had been

a magnet and victim to Narcissists my entire life. From my knowledge, I began counseling friends and co-workers. People would just share personal things with me, and I had this innate need to help them any way I could. So, I used my pain and past experiences coupled with my newfound knowledge of Narcissists, to help them.

As AcharYah explained the first 19 out of the 30 characteristics of a Narcissist, a light bulb went off in my head. "Anybody can have narcissistic traits, but if they have more than ten, they are a full-blown narcissist. Run!" I remember him saying. I wrote down each trait. The first thing I did was a self-analysis. But as he went into further description of each trait, I noticed that he was describing my friend's mother and her husband. It was blowing my mind. A detailed description of all 30 traits can be found in The Flight of the Narcissist written by Ausar Selassie Neteru, in Chapter Seven titled "30 Pieces of Silver." After that lesson, I called my friend to do further analysis of her situation. Below is a list of all 30 traits from the book that I focused on while I listened and noted her experiences:

1. *Incapable of dedicating themselves to something positive for the good of the whole for long periods of time.*
2. *Actions are dysfunctional even towards themselves.*
3. *Escape reality through vices.*
4. *Delusion of grandeur which is completely unsubstantiated.*
5. *Poor or great communicators.*
6. *Accomplishes very little or much but loses it all while blaming others.*

7. *The relationship is the sum-total of what you can do for them.*

8. *Their conscience speaks the language of selfishness and no other.*

9. *They are hypercritical.*

10. *They are hypersensitive.*

11. *They are hypocritical.*

12. *They present a fake morality that serves the purpose of getting them what they want through your guilt and shame.*

13. *They never believe themselves worthy of punishment nor truthfully and honestly admit that they have done wrong.*

14. *They are traitors and are disloyal, therefore, they will sell you out not simply to the highest bidder but even the lowest bidder or someone who makes no bid at all.*

15. *They are ungrateful.*

16. *They feed off your hurt feelings and negative emotions; they love to keep you upset.*

17. *They don't believe you are done with them until it's too late.*

18. *They are not accountable.*

19. *They lack organization.*

20. *They love drama, be it their own or others.*

21. *They create unnecessary problems.*

22. *They make blanket statements about society that are not grounded in reality as a means to justify their actions.*

23. *They make negative accusations of our being cynical based on incomplete or falsified historical and empirical evidence.*

24. *They make you the reason for their mistakes, mood, actions and personality glitches.*

25. *They are manic depressives.*
26. *They are vengeful.*
27. *Only masters can recognize a narcissist; others will not recognize narcissists in your live because their camouflage is superior.*
28. *Any advice only makes you an accuser and condemner; they ask for advice but any advice you give, they label as flawed.*
29. *They give the illusion of sanity therefore you treat them with respect and expect things from them for which they will constantly leave you disappointed.*
30. *They do things that are not needed and get angry when you ask for what is needed; they do for others what you need them to do for you.*

My analysis showed me that out of the thirty traits, she was a victim throughout her life from many different Narcissists that she encountered. After studying each trait carefully, I realized that her marriage showed signs of twenty of the thirty behaviors. I will discuss ten of those and give examples of what she endured up close. Remember, it only takes ten for the person to be considered a full narcissist versus just having narcissistic tendencies. The following is my analysis of ten of the traits:

The second trait, "Actions are Dysfunctional Even Towards Themselves", was present in her marriage. "With their pet projects, Narcissists select completely dysfunctional options that strain whatever relationship they have with you, whether it is financial, emotional or quality time. Whatever their business is will place a strain on the relationship" (Neteru, 2016, pg. 109). Her husband had his own business and she was his secretary and business partner. Along with her full-time job of nursing, she took on another part-time job just to make ends meet while she was helping him with his business. She often got calls from disgruntled clients who had not heard from him, including family and friends. He would not return phone calls or answer text messages, so they would call her. This led her to feel resentful towards him and the business. She was under a lot of stress and during some of this time, she was also pregnant. She spent most of the little free time she had supporting him.

The business never made that much. Or at least that is what she was told. The money from the business only contributed to food. He liked eating out even though it was not in their budget. Occasionally, he would pay, but most times he did not. Though, when they were around family or friends, she would pass him her debit card to pay the waiter, so it would look like he was paying for their meal. "In every area of the Narcissist's life we have been there to pick up the pieces, but they have never truly acknowledged that or been truly grateful. The worst part is that by doing this we enabled their dysfunction" (Neteru, 2016, pg. 109). She did this, so he could keep up the facade of being the "head of the family" and to not suffer embarrassment on his part or hers. Sometimes, to look more important, he would offer to pay for others without asking or consulting her. The lack of gratitude and consideration added to the resentment.

The next trait that I recognized right away was the third one: "Escape Reality Through Vices." Being a Service Engineer, her husband would always have the latest computers, tablets, phones, etc. Whenever he would update a tablet or phone, he would pass the old one down to her as a gift.

Narcissists present gifts or attention or kind words as though anything coming from them is special. Add it up. When you add up whatever a Narcissist gives you against the everyday glass house you have had to live in to get along with them, whatever they gave you is not enough much less too much. The truth is that in all their giving to you, they seldom give you what you need emotionally or possibly even financially. (Neteru, 2016, pg. 114)

He would wipe the memory of these devices and say that they are just like new. From her facial expressions and snide remarks, he knew that she did not like getting his "hand me downs." He would call her ungrateful and try to make her feel guilty. All the while, he was holding the latest version of whatever device he just gave to her.

The next characteristic is number four: "Delusion of Grandeur which is completely unsubstantiated." He wanted to maintain this image that he was completely on top of things. She told me about a time when they were struggling financially, and she could not pay the daycare bill. He was working, so she asked him for any financial help he could spare, and he told her he did not have any money. She had exhausted her entire income tax return buying him a truck because his car got repossessed. She had to beg the daycare to allow her children to keep going. One day when she got home from work, she noticed he was not home, but the truck was in the driveway. He came home driving a BMW. She was in shock. She explained the conversation that took place.

"What? What's this? Whose car is this?" she asked trying to figure out what was going on.

"It's mine. I just got it." He replied.

Pointing to the truck that was sitting in the driveway, she said, "A BMW? What's wrong with the truck?"

"It hasn't been working that well. I was spending all my money getting it fixed. I'm going to try to sell it."

"You can afford a car note? You said you couldn't help me with daycare. We owe them a lot of money." She was furious and could not believe he bought a car.

"I got a good deal. It's only $350.00 a month." He said with a wide grin.

From her description, he seemed completely oblivious to how that made her feel. He has never seen anything wrong with his decision. The car was ten years old and ended up giving him more trouble than the truck ever did. He took out a title loan on the truck and could not pay the loan back. The truck was taken. Not surprisingly, he lost his job and she had to help him pay the car note to prevent another repossession. And like always, she helped him. I started to see a pattern of behavior with both of them. With each experience she failed to communicate her disdain, thus enabling him to continue this behavior and feeding her resentment. "You see the Narcissist needs to believe that they are without flaw and that those with whom they associate are constantly in awe of them" (Neteru, 2016, pg. 118). All his friends or associates were vagabonds. They all looked up to him and thought he had the perfect life with the perfect family. "Narcissists put on a show that results in us believing that they are a magnificent person that we must get to know and/or in contrast they are a consummate victim that we must help" (Neteru, 2016, pg. 118). Her husband played both these roles. With his friends, he was a "god," but with her, he was the husband that needed his wife's support.

Trait five is: "Poor or Great communicators." For years, she thought she was going crazy. It was normal for her to have a conversation with her husband where they would come to some sort of agreement. Then, when she would bring it back up, he would completely deny what he said. Or he would say that she said something different. She felt that her memory had always been good, and she knew what they discussed, but he would be adamant. This drove her senseless and was extremely frustrating. "The reason that we get into communication paradigms of confusion, ambiguity, and frustration in dealing with Narcissists, is that Narcissists are either Poor or Great Communicators whose words in an argument are often the truth laced with lies" (Neteru, 2016, pg. 120). She explained that she wished that she had a recording device to prove that she was not losing her mind. Then she noticed that he did it with his siblings. She concluded that she was not the one that was crazy, he was.

> The Narcissist uses lying as both a defense mechanism and a control mechanism. While most people will use a lie to avoid retribution or punishment, the Narcissist will use lies to create false perception which leads others to a conclusion about them and their actions that is advantageous for them. (Neteru, 2016, pg. 122)

Her husband used lies throughout their marriage to set a false foundation in the beginning and to control her. When he would meet her extended family or old friends, he created a false occupation, would pretend to be in a Greek-lettered organization and lied about his level of education. However, he never did it in front of her. She would receive questions from people for verification or clarification. It put her in a very uncomfortable position. Once, her brother overheard one of his tall tells. He did this to impress people. The irony is that he was so intelligent, that he was believable.

The next characteristic I will discuss is number eleven: "They are Hypocritical." Throughout their entire marriage, people on the outside looking in thought they had the perfect family (including me). They got compliments all the time when they would be out in public. Couples would seek their advice and ask what was their secret to having a happy marriage, and they would give it. They both counseled couples all the time. He would talk to the husband and she would talk to the wife. Ironically, his advice was great, but he did not follow it at home. She put on a front and a smile like she was happy, but she was not. "What the public sees in terms of how the Narcissist takes care of home and the actual condition of the people in the home are two different things" (Neteru, 2016, pg. 145). They took family photos with great smiles. He played the part of the husband that took care of his family, was protective and made them feel safe. The truth was, she was taking care of their family and did not feel safe. After several sessions, I discovered that she was actually afraid of him. He had a temper that she cautioned not to trigger. He would say he hates domestic violence and would not even watch it on television, but she often felt that he was going to hit her. He has broken doors and put holes in walls. He has screamed and disempowered her. Nobody ever saw this side of him. In public, he came across as calm and peaceful. He kept a smile on his face and laughed all the time.

> Most people will never know that your Narcissist is a hypocrite. For example, in a domestic sense some Narcissists will assure that whatever is wrong at home will be fixed by the time their family is in front of people that they consider to be worthy of an opinion. (Neteru, 2016, pg. 144)

Apparently, he did not appear perfect in everybody's eyes. He did not see the owners of the daycare they were using as important. He disrespected them and her in front of them. One day, she got a call to pick up her daughter from daycare due to a reoccurring diaper rash. When she got home, Child Protective Services (CPS) was in the driveway. The CPS representative explained that they were being charged with serious allegations. She was shocked and did know where this was coming from. What surprised her was that her questions were all about her husband, not the children. The representative was trying to convince her that she was a victim of domestic violence and that her children were also being abused by her husband. The representative even asked would she be willing to leave him to keep her kids if it came to that. You see, he did not honor the opinion of the daycare; therefore, he did not put on that front of the perfect husband. They were cleared of any misconduct or abuse, but that line of questioning was perplexing for my friend. She realized that the daycare reported that the she and the children were being beaten and controlled.

The next two attributes I will deliberate are twelve and thirteen: "They Present A Fake Morality That Serves The

Purpose Of Getting Them What They Want Through Your Guilt And Shame" and "They Never Believe Themselves Worthy Of Punishment Nor Truthfully And Honestly Admit That They Have Done Wrong." From our discussions, I deduced that in her situation, these two traits go hand in hand. No matter how many disagreements they had or how many times she would prove him wrong, he could never admit it. The church they attended was starting new after school programs to help students in Reading and Math. The first lady approached my friend and asked would she be willing to help tutor. After learning that this would be consistent income, she agreed. Instead of being happy for her, her husband was upset about this because he was not offered pay for helping with the church website. He would complain about the church and other members. Describing a fake morality, it says, "You will also find that Narcissists use the tactic of speaking negatively about things that you are connected to but not directly about you" (Neteru. 2016, pg. 149). He would offer ideas on how to help from a technology standpoint. He felt they were living in the dark ages. He protested that he was not being heard. These people were her family and had become dear friends. She said it was hard to listen to the negative talk.

Although he continued to criticize, she later learned on accident that he was being paid by the church to maintain their website. So, she asked him straight out if he was being compensated, and he said no. He then proceeded to complain and slander the church even more. It was clear he did not want her to know that he had additional income because he did not want to be asked to help more with the bills. From never believing themselves worthy of punishment, "You literally have to be psychic to discern that they are being so completely dishonest with you. The Narcissists will lie with a straight face and even brag about how great it feels to be in synergy with you" (Neteru, 2016, pg. 152). If she had not known the truth, she would have never known he was lying. I could see that she was more bothered that he was able to lie to her face with such ease than the fact that he was hiding money. This not only added to her resentment, but she no longer trusted him. Once again, she did not let him know that she knew he was lying, thus enabling him further to continue in his behavior.

Although I felt our talks were helping her, at this time I was no expert. I was a good listener and someone she could vent too. I was also showing her from my own teachings how his behavior resembled that of a narcissist. When she told me that her church offered marriage counseling, I advised her to ask him if he would be willing to go. Even with the truth, she wanted to desperately save her marriage. He agreed to counseling and they started seeking counsel to help in areas where I could not. The main issue that was discussed was the difference in the way they viewed finance and her disdain for his lack of help. It was suggested that he let her take over all the bills and that he give her a lump sum every month from his paycheck to help toward the bills. They both agreed to this, and it was working out well for about three months. Then he just stopped after she filed for the income tax return. She usually put this money aside to use for travel and family vacations during the summer. It was not supposed to be for their daily bills. When she asked why he stopped contributing, he said, "You got money." Around this same time, her debit card got hacked and she had to get a new one. She had to set up her automatic bill pay all over again. This time, she set it up to come out of her checking account versus the debit card to prevent ever having to redo this. She was trying to save up for the kids to go visit family out of town and noticed that her balance was lower than it should be. She could not tell why, so she went to the bank. She asked about everything that was coming out each month and anything additional. The banker explained that she had one bill coming from her debit card. She thought he was mistaken, because she purposely did not have any bills coming from this card. I remember discussing this with her. After her card got hacked, it was best to have bills come straight out of the bank account. So, she asked what the bill was. He explained that it was a T-Mobile phone bill. Her phone was with AT&T. However, her husband's phone was with T-Mobile. This was strange to her because she never gave him her new card or agreed to pay his phone bill. At this time, he was working, and she thought he was paying his own bills. This meant that he went into her bag, took the card out and set up the payments. Her husband was stealing from her. I advised her to close out that card and get a new one. I told her that she should just ask him about it and to not jump to conclusions. When she asked him about this, he said she allowed it. He never admitted to stealing her card. He believed it was okay to stop helping with bills because he knew she had extra money from income tax. He thought that it was okay to steal her debit card to have his personal phone bill paid every month. He had a full-time job and did not think anything was wrong with putting everything on his wife. This clearly was not the agreement they made.

The next persona is: "They Don't Believe That You Are Done With Them Until It's Too Late." After being married thirteen years and giving birth to four children, she forgave and forgave and forgave. She explained that she took vows: for

better or worse. She did not want to become part of that divorce statistic. I completely understood that. None of us get married thinking one day it will end in divorce. Once you have children, most of us really try to make it work. To help her marriage, she started working on her appearance. However, he stopped paying attention to her. She would get manicures, pedicures, eyebrows done, lingerie- all just to try and get his attention. Unfortunately, he never noticed. "You were never valuable enough for them to pay attention to you when you were there. They didn't care what happened to the children or even how you were surviving, because they did not care about you" (Neteru, 2016, pg. 163). When she brought it up, he just compared it to her not noticing his new mug that he had in his office- a room she seldom went in. She tried to explain to him that noticing her, a person, his wife, was totally different from her noticing a cup. This may sound crazy, but it is true. This was a real argument. I could not believe it at first. They also argued about the care of their children. She had three sons that needed haircuts at least every two weeks. She was the one that always took them, but she asked him to do it. She felt this was something that the father should do with his sons. Not to mention, she felt uncomfortable going to those barber shops around all those men. He did not seem to care about her discomfort or the boys being well-groomed. He said that they did not need to get haircuts because he did not get haircuts when he was a boy. Again, this did not make sense. He grew up in a single parent home and his mother could not afford to get him consistent haircuts. She wondered why should their sons suffer and be made fun of. Thus, she just continued to take them herself. I could clearly see that all of this was just pushing her further and further away. As an Ascended Master, my eyes were open, and I could see that she was dealing with a Narcissist.

I did my best to just share my teachings so she could see it for herself.

Next, we have: "They Make You The Reason For Their Mistakes, Mood, Actions And Personality Glitches." As before mentioned, she helped him with his business when he was not working, however, he always found a way to blame her for all his shortcomings. He said that his failures and limitations were due to her negative mindset. He said that it was her thoughts that caused him to lose his jobs and any financial struggle they had. When she would express worry over their bills while he would splurge, he would say that she was being negative. Her worry was coming from a place of remembering their lights getting cut off, water getting cut off, not having hot water, etc.- all due to him not paying the bills he was responsible for. "How in the hell can you blame a woman who has carried a man for 12 years for leaving him when he pays no attention to her, does not help with the children, and pays no bills? You can't" (Neteru, 2016, pg. 187). After showing her this and our many sessions, it gave her the courage to finally walk away. I was careful not to ever advise that she leave, just show her so she could discover it on her own. When she finally left, people thought she was crazy. She did not advertise her treatment or disdain. She had reached a breaking point and could not take it anymore. Regrettably, she was made to feel like she did something wrong. "Did he hit you? Did he cheat on you? Is he on drugs?" These are the questions people would ask, and when she said "no" or "not that I know of" as an answer, they would frown and looked perplexed. She finally realized that all the years of enabling him and pretending they had this seamless family, backfired. All their judgments came

from expectations of the Social Fantasy- something she was no longer interested in keeping up with.

The last attribute I will talk about is: "Only Masters Can Recognize A Narcissist, Others Will Not Recognize Narcissists In Your Life Because Their Camouflage Is Superior." For her, this trait was the hardest one to deal with. You see, her husband took drama in high school and I was told that he was very good. This talent coupled with his intelligence made his camouflage undetectable. He had just about everybody fooled, and still does. She explained that when they first met, he was not a fan of football and never watched it. When they started going to their church, it was evident that the men there all loved football, had favorite teams and was really into it. They would talk about it after service. He eagerly joined the conversations, claiming to be a Texans fan. He chose this team because he was from Houston. She was surprised because she knew he did not care for the sport at all. He then went home and began doing research on the history of the Texans. He then started a Fantasy Football game with the men at the church. He even went so far as to purchase a T-Shirt as the prize for the winner. Wait, there is more. He bought the whole family Texans Jerseys and they took family photos. He still didn't really watch the games; he would just look up the highlights afterwards. "One of our greatest frustrations is that other people do not see what we see in the Narcissist" (Neteru, 2016, pg. 194). She was in awe of his performance. There were even times she forgot that it was all an act. What's even more interesting is that they both really became Texans fans.

In the end, she finally learned that what they had was not real. Many of us ask the question, "Who did I marry? How much

of himself is really him?" when the person we dated is totally different from the person we took vows with. This leads to confusion, frustration and just being plain unhappy. To no surprise, my friend cried almost every day.

> A wife/husband is one who is hopefully a soul mate but at the very least a life partner with whom we share synergetic compatibility which means our nature, cosmic elements, affinities, and destinies comfortably align in a way that produces Peace, Harmony and Balance. (Neteru, 2016, pg. 24)

I believe the lesson we both learned is the importance of taking our time to truly getting to know someone before committing to marriage. We should not allow ourselves to be victims to pressure because we are getting older, or even we must marry because we got pregnant. Pregnancy is not a good reason to marry someone you hardly know. Learning your purpose in life and learning to love yourself will help you attract somebody who is a reflection of you. We only put up with what we subconsciously think we deserve. Yes, my friend's husband had many faults, but with each example of a narcissistic trait, she enabled him. This was a result of a lack of self-love. Focus on "liking" someone and unfeignedly feeling a connection. Below is a poem I wrote on what I think that connection could feel like:

Synergy

Your imperfections are my blessings on a new day
I bring you close with my meditation to have you my way
I wish to lay at your feet and climb your wisdom of truth
Two decades of minimal energy exchange
Yet I always felt you
Pretty browns piercing through my soul
Waking up my spirit self
My true self
We have this powerful connection that I can't comprehend
Your image implanted on my soul to no end
Your gaze touches me thru your photo and kisses my forehead
Your voice distracts me from my stress -my depression is dead
We suspend time and space whenever we speak on the phone
Words touch my heart chakra and come out as song
Your being is congealed with my energy
On every level I feel we are in synergy

Chapter 11:

Psychic Ability

What is Psychic Ability or having the ability to listen to that inner voice? Many people wonder if they possess Psychic Abilities. Believe it or not, everyone is psychic to some degree. We all can tap into another vibration and gain entry to universal information that will help escort us through life. I liken this skill to having a direct connection to universal consciousness that permits us to see and hear visions of the past, present, and future and discover what secrets they hold. Some people even have the capability to link to a place I like to call "The other side." This is a place (often referred to as heaven) beyond the shroud that we enter after our soul leaves the physical world. People who have this ability can connect with those who have passed on in order to receive and convey messages from the spirits of loved ones. My sister and paternal grandparents have this gift. When we are born with this level of psychic ability, no matter how much we try to ignore it, it will keep coming back and pushing us to learn more about this gift. Education and the craving to expand our range of knowledge, is an influential persuader in and of itself. Combine that yearning for education with psychic energy waiting to be released, and inquisitiveness quickly turns to a requirement to learn more about ourselves.

Subsequently, let's start our journey of discovery by defining "psychic ability"? Psychic Ability is our mind and body reading and acknowledging the energy and vibrations that

surround us every day. This capacity exists in many different categories; from the traditional expectations of predicting the future to being intuitive (knowing) or even being a medium (speaking to the dead). These are all the ways you can listen to your inner soul to receive the answers you seek. Psychiatrists, therapists, psychologists and counselors are there to help guide those who are lost and have lost the ability to hear that voice. With psycho-energetic counseling and energy healing, you can unblock your chakras and begin to hear again. Moments of connection with our inner skills may appear as a gut feeling about the future, premonitions through dreams, or seeing spirits walk through the house. Our psychic abilities differ from person to person. Everyone has been provided their own unique way to tap into their hidden power. Psychic abilities are broken down into 3 basic classifications: clairvoyance (Clear Seeing) which is the ability to see, clairsentience (Clear Sensing) which is the ability to feel, and Clair cognizance (Clear Knowing) which is the ability to know. We use all three of these capacities when performing a psychic reading, tapping into psychic vibration or listening to your soul. Everyone has had at least one experience or encounter with one of these categories sometime in their life. Although all of us are able with the suitable direction to use all three of these senses, the ordinary person will have just one that is their major or strongest sense that will be developed the most.

Whether we realize it or not, we all have the internal capability to find the answers we need to handle any given situation. Normally referred to as being intuitive or cognitive, this extraordinary gift allows us to open our senses, so we can hear, see, feel and understand on a deeper level the unexpected situations that appear in our lives. I call this listening to your soul. This ability will always be there to help us find comfort

and light through any struggle and provide the guidance needed to enhance our lives. To help you to understand more about this skill, let me take you back to my life as a child. I grew up being very sensitive to the energy of others. Psychic ability also runs in my family- from my sister, grandmother and grandfather to a touch of it in myself. As a little girl, I did not know what I was feeling or seeing or even sometimes smelling. Many times, I thought I was having vivid dreams because I could not make sense of what I was seeing.

At the age of five, I remember my schoolmates in my kindergarten class. As I met each one, I could feel energy from them that would either drain me or give to me. I learned to be around those that gave me energy or had bright spirits as opposed to those children that would make me feel tired or weak. I later learned that this form of psychic ability is called being an Emotional Empath. I could sense things about people that I never knew if it was real or in my imagination. There was a boy in my class who was adopted. I knew that this did not bother him, but he was not happy. I knew that his father drank a lot and would hit his mother. I knew that that marriage would not last. I knew that he would choose a life that would lead down a dark path. I could also feel that he was a good person deep down and was just a little boy in pain. I felt all of this from him from kindergarten to sixth grade. I silently worried about him. My mother moved us away and I lost touch with him. But I later discovered that everything I felt about him was true. During his teen years, he was in and out of jail for robbery and drug dealing. He barely missed being sentenced to life in prison for his third strike. The judge showed him mercy. He is now out and has gone back to school. He gave his first sermon after being out for a few months. His mother and father are divorced, and his father is a

recovering alcoholic. I had no idea that those fragments I saw in my mind would come true. Sometimes I wondered if I was crazy. I was very good at hiding and not speaking of what I was feeling.

I also knew that my best friend at that time would never have children. It was like fragments of broken glass in my head-always just a feeling. I later described these feelings as "vibes" and I stopped seeing the fragments. All I had left were the vibes and feeling what others felt. I would ignore it and push it to the back of my mind until I no longer could "see" into the lives of others, but I could still "feel" what other people felt as if I had gone through it myself.

Late at night, I would see a small man dressed in black and white stripes resembling a dwarf of some kind. He would run through the halls of the house and hide around corners. I would just sit up in my bed and watch him. He would look at me and laugh. The next morning, I would assume I was dreaming and never spoke of him. It was not until I was an adult talking to my sister about my different experiences that I realized he was real. She saw him too. We both discovered that what we saw as children in our home and places where we spent the night, were real. I remember my parents dropped us off at a friend's house to be baby sat and we were to spend the night. They had a huge grey Great Dane that looked like a horse to me. It was the biggest dog I had ever seen. The room I slept in opened to a long hallway that led to a side door that led to outside. That night, there was a different small man dressed like a joker. He was very short and round. He wore a hat like the joker with bells on it. He was in the room tickling me and laughing. He sprinkled dust in my eyes. I asked him who he was, and he said that he was the sand man. He strolled down the hall, opened the side door and left. Again, I thought that I was dreaming. This was another shared

memory with my sister. She saw the same little man and remembered what he said. The following morning when I woke up, my eyes were crusty. Throughout my own life, I heard the voice. I always had that feeling that someone was watching over me. And when I did not listen, bad things happened.

In late April of 2013, my sister had an experience on a Sunday and a Monday. It was right after her birthday. Circles of light appeared on her walls and ceiling. Some were purple, others were white. There were even some that were rainbow. The amazing thing is that she could hear them. When I went to visit her a few days later, she asked if they would come back so I could see them, and they told her yes. As soon as I arrived, I was about to sit down to eat when she came out the room and yelled, "They're back! They came for you! I asked them to come and they came." I immediately took out my iPad to record the amazing lights. It was like a light show. First, I saw a rainbow stream above my sister's picture with one white circle on the ceiling above the same picture. This was the picture on her husband's altar. Then, the purple lights appeared. They were small circles arranged in an arc, then a straight line like a sickle. I told them thank you for coming. I felt honored. It was intriguing. Round rainbow circles appeared on the ceiling above the ceiling fan. Then there were flickering lights on another wall. All the lights would fade in and out. It started about 8:15 am. Which was the same time they came on the previous days. This time, her closet and bathroom door were open. Energy imprints were left in both places, plus all over the wall of the room. These imprints were like light streaks on the wall and /or oil spots. When things calmed down around 9 am, my sister took a shower. When she came out, that's when she noticed spots on the wall. I took pictures. Then they started to fade, and I took

more pictures for the before and after affect. My sister took her wedding ring from her altar and put it on. Then she went back into the bathroom. She came out and said a light was coming from her ring into the mirror. I urged her to go back so I could film it. Reluctantly, she agreed. She put her fist up with the ring facing the mirror. A white circle of light appeared and began dancing on the mirror. She kept her hand still. Then she saw a flash of light zip past her. But the light remained on the mirror. This only lasted a few minutes. Before she took the shower, we noticed that all the candles on her altar had gone out. There was no more wax in them. However, when we came out of the bathroom, the tea candle in front of the Deity Het-Heru (Hathor) was re-lit. It was weird because there was no wax- just a wick. We tripped out. I figured it was the Deity Het-Heru (Hathor) sending a message. My sister had dreamed about her a few days prior. I wish I could hear them too, so I could help my sister. She couldn't sleep for about a week after the first sighting. In fact, it was several days before she slept through the night. They told her they had work to do. She was afraid of her mission and her gifts.

Chapter 12:

Emotional Empath

From researching my sensitivity, I discovered that I am an Emotional Empath. Judith Orloff goes into depth on what an Empath is and what it means. It is one of the Emotional Energy types that I studied. The following quiz is found in Orloff's book, Positive Energy.

Quiz: Am I An Intuitive Empath:

Ask Yourself:

- Have I been labeled as overly sensitive?
- If a friend is distraught or in physical pain, do I start feeling it too?
- Am I drained in crowd, going out of my way to avoid them?
- Do I get anxious in packed elevators, airplanes, or subways?
- Am I hypersensitive to noise, scents, or excessive talking?
- When I see gruesome newscasts, does my energy plummet?
- Do I get burned out by groups, requires lots of time alone to revive? (Orloff, 2004, p. 29)

I answered yes to all these questions. Empathy, for many of us, is the ability to imagine, identify with, and feel compassion for another's expressed emotional or physical circumstance. It is through the gift of Empathy we can internalize the feelings of others. We can relate to the sorrow

that comes with the passing of a loved one and touch that mix of emotions provoked by a failed relationship. Each of us can feel great compassion for those experiencing the emotional and physical pain brought on by a disease such as cancer. It is easy to embrace the sadness, anguish and despair that come to an abused child. Empathy also plays a role in the deep connection between mother and child and mother's intuition. It is how we know when family needs us, no matter how near or far away they may be. The gift of Empathy also allows us to share in a multitude of positive energies. We will vicariously live the joy and excitement of a co-worker who achieves that long-awaited promotion. Memories and dreams awaken, and desire peaks as we share in the exhilaration of the bride and groom on their wedding day. The Empathic connection lends support to the feelings of want, desire and need we experience for our lover, partner, husband, wife or friend. Our feelings, thoughts and life experiences are our essence. They become part of our life force, stored in our aura and emitted as either negative or positive energies into the universe. That process allows our realities to be easily accessed by everyone we meet. Our vulnerabilities and strengths are displayed for the determinations and judgment of others. They know our intimate truths through the energies we emit and are privy to information we do not intend to share. Each connection we make offers a certain level of insight, awareness and sensitivity to the people we meet.

Empathy provides easy access to our inner being in a short span of time. It is how we feel the sincerity and intent in another. Empathy allows us to detect the 'good vibes' in another or sense the 'bad vibes'. It awakens the intuition. We connect with their life force and enter their personal inner space, if only to graze the outer edges for a moment in passing. The ability to

sense or feel another's energy is part of our core design and the Empathic process. It is not a role, which can be calculated or demanded. Empathy is a natural, unsolicited response that is born in us all. Consciously or unconsciously, we connect empathically with our fellow man. It is spiritual in nature and links us as one in the universe. For some, the connection to the energies of others is felt with great intensity and depth. Our intuitive capabilities and Empathy have life. As highly sensitive individuals, we have the capability to move past the vicarious experiences into a virtual reality. Our heightened awareness allows us to absorb the experiences of another, be in the moment with them, and live the actual emotions and physical conditions of others. We will wear the sorrow, apprehensions, pains, troubles or euphoria of another, as our own.

Empathy, at this level, is ever present and provokes a continuously charged state of being. Those who carry this level of Empathy are known as an Empath or Intuitive. According to the experts, this gift comes with a specific purpose. The designated role is to help humanity and clear the earth of emotional clutter. The Empath connects to the light of others through the senses, the mind, body, soul, spirit, intellect and sexual energies. We can know another's mindset and heart through body language, voice tone, a glance or in a slight touch. An Empath can feel the energies stored in the aura of another through incidental contact or in passing. Most all Empaths receive the vibes emitted by others because of the melding process that takes place as our energies travel through the Universe. It involves that which can be seen, as well as the unseen.

This gift is not limited to identifying with the emotions and pain of one's situation. It is a deeper, far-reaching, on-going

and more intense union with the essence of another. There is debate regarding the onset of this gift, however. Some claim we are born to it, while others are sure anyone can develop these talents, at any given time in life. Others believe we are contracted before taking our earthly presence, to serve a specific purpose. We are given the task of helping humanity, ridding the earth of excess emotion. Most of the experts share in the belief that we are born as Empaths without control or contract to our calling. Those who believe it can be cultivated later in life do admit it may have been there for years, but not awakened or recognized until a later time.

Each Empath receives and manifests his gift in a different form or in all forms and with varying degrees of intensity. One Empath may be adept in realizing and internalizing one's physical condition. For example, many times, I will feel ill and will later learn that I have the exact symptoms of someone close to me or a family member. Another Empath will know a person's emotional condition and its accompanying realities. One day when dropping my daughter off at daycare, I briefly touched her caregiver and immediately felt this overwhelming pain in my chest. I felt sad, disheartened and disappointed. A gallon of tears rolled down my cheeks as I drove to work. I was having a hard time catching my breath. When I got to work, people thought that I was having an asthma attack, but when my vitals were checked, I was fine (medically). There was no proof of an asthma attack. I later learned that the caregiver had just had a devastating argument with her husband that morning. She passed those emotions right to me. So, it seems I have both forms.

Some Empaths might gain a deep connection to our spiritual essence or hold a more acute response to our aura. They

can touch the darkest part of us that no one knows, and the average person could never reach. Some find their gift in a connection to plant life, trees, animals, a place, an object, entities or nature spirits, such as angels and ferries. An Empath's sensitivities and openness to all energies make us more keenly aware of our environment. We are immediately touched by the 'vibes' and is physically and/ or emotionally affected by the energies present. Upon entering the auric space of a building or town, we can feel the residing energies. In my own personal experience, I went through this when I was looking for a house. I was meeting a realtor to see a house and he had left the key, so I could get in. As soon as I walked in the house, my chest tightened, and I felt afraid. I wanted to run out and hide. I felt that someone had hid in the closet fearing for their life. This feeling was strong and overwhelming. I clutched my chest and tears started rolling down my cheeks. I got out of there fast. I was crying uncontrollably and could not stop. I did not understand what I was feeling or why I was crying. I left the house and parked at a nearby store to try and clam myself down. Later, I researched the home and saw pictures of it boarded up along with that yellow crime tape. Something bad had happened there and I could feel it.

An entire town can have 'bad vibes' as a result of the amount of negative energy accumulated by its residents, spirits, animal inhabitants, buildings and trees. I experience this daily when I pass through a certain small-town driving to work. At the same point each day, a draining feeling comes over me, and I feel weak and tired. My head hurts and my chest would tighten up. At first, I attributed it to not enough sleep, but I realized it happened at the exact same spot every day. I would feel fine and fully awake when I start my day until I get to the entrance of a

particular town. It is not as much a negative feeling as it is draining. Some days, I must stop at a gas station to get a beverage and walk around. I find that grounding myself helps restore my energy.

An Empath can feel the negative or positive vibrations in the air. We all have heard the expression: "This place gives me the creeps." It is like when we meet someone, shake their hand, and immediately get a bad feeling. We cannot explain it, but we know this person's energy is not in synergy with our own. Large doses of negative energy, entering our being at once, will have a profound affect. Without warning, it can present an overwhelming attack of physical and/ or emotional pain for the Empath. The power of this collective negative energy can be devastating. The Empath may experience unexplained panic, fear or pain. Not knowing the source of those unexplained feelings can be frightening. Many of us have been affected by that type of collective, negative energy or felt welcomed by overwhelming positive energies. We all remember that feeling when we walk in grandma's house or that favorite aunt- the smell of home cooking and the air that feels like a warm hug. Those are the positive energies. There are some homes that just "feel" good to be in. This is the energy that feeds us. As energy is emitted from the aura, it travels and melds in the universe, making it accessible and formidable.

Being an Empath can also mean being an open portal for connections with life on the other side. Those who have passed seek a gateway through which their voices may be heard, and the Empath becomes the likely source. If the Empath is not aware, he/ she can become overcome by the many attempts to interconnect. Halloween, Thanksgiving and Christmas are especially difficult times due to an increase in spirit activity. The

call for a connection between worlds is high. The Empath can feel as if there is a revolving door to and from the other world displaying a flashing neon sign, which reads: "Open. Come in here." We will have to consciously, with great effort, close the portal and change the sign to read, "No Admittance-Out of order." The Empath's receptors are always in the on position allowing a continuous flow of delicate to dangerous energies to enter our personal space. We must contend with the flow of outside energy as well as his own, and sort those, which belong to him. Asking an Empath how he/she feels can be a loaded question, which requires great effort to answer. We must examine through and separate others' agony and emotional drama before we can know how we feel. The life of an Empath requires that we consciously work to tune out and turn off the flow of those outside influences, in order to be aware of our own state of being. Empaths must find ways to protect their energy.

Regrettably, far too many Empaths live in excess, feeling off balance and out of control. They become lost to the spasms of stress and suffer an energy overdose. Because Empathy is at the core of their being, the challenges can have a reflective effect on how they view and manage their day-to-day lives. A trip to the grocery store, going to the mall or simply watching a movie or TV show can turn into a major event, which changes the course of their day. Because of this, I no longer watch the news and seldom watch television. I prefer to shop online and do not like large crowds. I must be very careful what I allow in my energy field. Our ability to collect negative energy at every turn, presents us an unpredictable, insecure world without the benefit of knowing which encounter will incite insanity. Because of the many challenges, some Empaths see their gift as a curse. The negatives can be overwhelming, confusing and frustrating. For

those unaware of their gift, life can be an agonizing journey. The Empath may isolate themselves and feel alone or crazy, without the comfort of understanding and answers. Many seek solutions to their emotional overload through therapy; believing they are responsible for their condition. Others try to make it go away by losing themselves in drugs or alcohol, numbing the senses so as not to feel. Neither of those options provides a viable solution.

The Empathic gift brings many positive opportunities as well. Helping others heal is at the top of the list. They can know what you are feeling even when you don't. They will have answers for the unasked questions. The Empath can understand what others cannot and are able to see what others can't see. They can avert costly mistakes or harmful incidents if they pay attention. As a bonus, their sexual experiences are intensified, spiritual awakenings. They can travel to the deepest, darkest places within their partner, creating a more meaningful experience. Empathy comes with no instruction manual and is not something with which the general population can easily identify. Doctors can offer no help and there is no cure. No one to this point has all the answers and no one could provide us solutions. This is a personal and individual journey. Each Empath must find his own methods for obtaining relief and staving off the negative light of others. Whatever works for the Empath is the right choice. There are materials published by and for Empaths, which can offer insight and advice for perfecting and coping with Empathy and fresh ideas are welcomed. There is help available and there are solutions and positives. Some may find that difficult to fathom considering the many challenges, but there are great positives that come with our gift as well. It is in our best interest to focus on the benefits of having this special gift and the talents that come with it. We must learn to use

Empathy to our best advantage and not let the challenges dictate who we become. Regardless of our adventures, trials and tribulations, it is important to understand that we are not crazy or alone. We are Empaths. We are special people who are allowed fabulous opportunities that others do not get to experience.

While the Empath is born to his/her gift, not all are aware of its presence or power. As children, we do not notice we are different and are not aware we possess any special talents. We see Empathy as normal life. Unfortunately, our parents have no way to know who we are and in the early years we don't understand our role as an Empath or the major impact it will hold in our future. "Discovering you're an empath can be a revelation. Putting a name to a very real intuitive experience legitimizes your perceptions. It also pinpoints where you're losing energy, so you can regain it" (Orloff, 2004, p. 29). Psycho-energetic techniques have helped me learn to protect myself against what Orloff calls Energy Vampires.

> How do you know if you've encountered a vampire?
> The tip-off is that even after a brief contact you leave feeling worse, but he or she seems more alive...
> Always realize that there's a difference between bad chemistry with someone, which simplify doesn't feel good, and being drained, when energy is taken from you. (Orloff, 2004, P. 290)

Energy Vampires can be likened to the narcissists in our lives. This is an added attribute. Growing up, I had no idea what I was feeling half the time and have just recently learned how to cope. Whether we are chosen or receive our gift by accident, it makes us unique and provides an amazing journey.

Chapter 13

Healing Through Psycho Energetic Counseling

The type of pain and trauma I have endured forms blocks- as long as we dwell in it instead of delving on it, it will control us and block us from our greatness. We are all great! Best believe that! So, how do we get passed the pain? I'm glad you asked. Are you ready to take a journey with me? A journey toward your purpose in life- your greatness. I hope my words will trigger that God within to shout so you can hear her; she's been talking to you for a long time. I will show you how to listen. The following is how I started my healing process through psycho energetic counseling- a process that never ends.

Manifestation Work: I found a space in my room where I could set up an altar with the idea of sacred geometry. I used frankincense to clean out dark energies. I was advised not to mix frankincense with sage. I then lit the actual frankincense, not the coal so I could determine the magnitude of the dark energy. This is best done is a saucepan. I paid attention to the time and intensity of the flame on the frankincense. When burning it, you must leave a door or window open and tell all the dark energies to leave. This will cleanse the area and anyone in the room. I got a white candle that did not have a scent. This was to magnify my power and can be used as a focal point during meditation. If the candle burns black soot, there is something heavy in the room. It was important to watch the flame as much as possible and to not blow it out. My prayer must be very specific. For example, I had to decide which problem I would want to focus on first:

financial stability or health. These were my main two issues that have been the result of a value system that was disempowering. The more specific, the easier it is for the universe to give it to me. I needed a focused and consistent manifestation. Any elements on the altar must be organic. Depending on my focused manifestation, I would need to know the right time, season, month, and moon phase, day of week and time of day to manifest. I looked at my physical schedule to see when to take the day off. I could not stress or mix it with my daily activities. Next, I wrote down my intention. I researched and choose colors, herbs and stones that corresponded with my intention. It is also beneficial to fast the day of the ritual. I asked permission from my spirit guide, Maát. I then made a list of everything I needed for the ritual. I handpicked each item and purified these items with sea salt under a full moon. I dedicated the space and cast a circle. Next, I stated my purpose for the space, "I consecrate this space." I said this 9 times. I ended the ritual with, "And so it is." I learned that I should not keep the items used in the ritual; dispose of it a certain way by burying them or throwing them in the ocean. To act in accordance to my ritual, I did my best not to speak negativity back into my life. The universe knows exactly what you really want. I knew that my lifestyle would reveal my true intentions. Two herbs I used were Life Everlasting, which is for health and longevity; and Mother's Wort, which is family protection and helps build trust in relationships in the household.

Figure 29: Chakra Stones for Your Altar

Happiness: Humans have six major needs. They need to have connections or bonds that go beyond love. Humans need sustenance. This should not be confused with money. The less you need to live on, the less control the Social Fantasy has over you. The third thing humans need is variety; doing the same thing all the time gets boring. They also need to have a growth plan. The 5th need is significance. Making contributions without recognition is being used. People need to be validated so they are empowered; they need and want recognition that is meaningful. The 6th need is stimulation, which are things we need to de-stress. We have been taught that stimulation is evil, so we should not indulge. The result is that we either hide from it or over-indulge. People will focus on stimulation when the other needs are not being met. This leads to hobbies, habits and addictions. The job of the Corporate Ego is to stop giving and receiving of these needs. Our satisfaction levels depend on how many needs are met. My goal was to increase my level of satisfaction by first making myself aware. I began to analyze my past and journal about any past traumas. I had to revisit each trauma in my life and recycle those memories to make them stepping-stones for my future. From awareness, we would move to tolerance and gratitude. From there, the next level of satisfaction is pleasure, then fulfillment and lastly, functionality. Once I reach functionality, this is the "happy zone."

Relationship Work: I had to discuss the kinds of people that would hinder my growth, so I could identify who I needed to distance myself from. My divorce was the first step in this work. There are three kinds of people that will interrupt me while I am making a life change. The first type is a Hypocrite. These people stand in opposition to their own statements by being the antithesis of what they say. The second kind are Users, which are people that are selfish and create a plan of life that continually use your resources to get done what they want. The third kind of person is a Liar. Liars are cowards who seek to avoid the consequences of their actions, while attaining all the benefits of someone who did it right. All these people could also be Narcissists, which we discovered is a person who is obsessively and excessively preoccupied with personal adequacy, power, prestige, and vanity to the extent that they have been completely closed to Dharma and completely reliant on the dark forces of the Corporate Ego. I made a list of the people in my life and determined if any of them fit these criteria. Next, was changing my job. I was surrounded by these types of people. I decided to only engage in relationships that empowered me. All traumas and stress come through relationship. However, all progress and access also come through relationship. The best way to deal with a Narcissist is toning and spiritual technologies.

The bottom line is to reach peace, harmony and balance. I had to make the choice to be invisible or invincible, victim or victor. The universe does not support disempowering goals or

continued victimization. The universe will give you abilities directly correlated to your goal, determination to reach that goal, and challenge. Every challenge builds your external divine energy. If I do the work, the universe will back me up.

One of the biggest contributors to my trauma was being betrayed by people I loved and trusted. Betrayal is when you break a covenant that we have established. It is when you sell someone out that does not deserve or expect it. We can't prevent it and we should not try to impress them. Why do people betray? Jealousy is the number one reason. Jealousy is when someone is energetically disturbed by your success. Envy is when that turns from inward to outward expression. They plant seeds of deceit amongst those who are with you; they sabotage your reputation and or work to keep you down. They align themselves with your enemy. Judas sold Jesus out for the price of a slave. Jealousy and envy are ugly states of self-destruction. Another reason people betray is insecurity, which is the mother of jealousy and envy. This is a blocked state of mind and is very dangerous. Resentment is the third reason someone will betray you. This is toxic memorization. It is not the action, but how it made you feel; this is born out of unexpressed, repressed emotion. They will keep sending you the message repeatedly, which will cause you to become bitter.

The following are the results of my BWEI, performed by Disciple Kafale Baker of the Self-Empowerment Center:

The Bio-Vibrational Wheel of Element Identification (BWEI)

FIRE (2,7)		WATER (1,6)		EARTH (0,5)		MINERAL (4,9)		NATURE (3,8)	
2	7	1		0	5	4	9	3	8
2		1		0	5	4	9		8
2		1			5	4	9		8
2		1			5		9		
2		1			5		9		
		1			5				
		1			5				
		1			5				
		1			5				
		1							
		1							
		1							
		1							
		1							
		1							
		1							
		1							
5	1	17	0	2	9	3	5	1	3
6		17		11		8		4	

MALE (0-4)	FIRE	WATER	EARTH	MINERAL	NATURE	TOTAL			
	5	17	2	3	1	28			

FEMALE (5-9)	FIRE	WATER	EARTH	MINERAL	NATURE	TOTAL			
	1	0	9	5	3	18			

Figure 30: BWEI for Kirsten Westbrook

183

Spiritual/Life Purpose

Your purpose is designated by the last number in the year you were born. In my case, 5 is the last number in 1975; meaning earth was the dominate element in universe at the time of my birth. Therefore, I am an earth spirit. I symbolize the mother, home, nourishment, support, comfort, empowerment, rootedness and centeredness. The earth doesn't judge. It provides care for all under her purview.

My medicine wheel revealed that I have 6 fire energies and 17 water energies. Fire and Water are the most potent of the five elements. There is a three to one ratio of water to fire since fire is the more dominate energy of the two. This means to be balanced, I need to have three times more water than fire. I have only one less from being completely balanced between fire and water because six times three is eighteen and I have seventeen. My chart reveals that I have 11 earth energies meaning I have an abundance of energy in this area. The spiritual gift of the earth is nurturing and providing for those in need. I have 8 mineral energies offering me a wealth of energy in this element. Mineral energy is the place of spiritual knowledge. I have 4 nature energies which means I have balanced energy in this element.

Three energies in each element are necessary to provide completion in a given element so that I can access the spiritual gifts associated with a given element. I have more than three with each element. The exception is water as one will typically have more water so as to balance their fire. An imbalance in any element blocks you from fully maximizing your purpose or tuning into the spiritual gifts associated with a given element. I also need a balance of fire and water to effectively access the spiritual gifts associated with earth, nature and mineral.

Male and Female Energy

You need three times more male energy than female energy to create a balance between the two energies. Feminine energy is more potent than male energy.

Feminine energy: It's nurturing, creative, intuitive and caring. It grants us the opportunity to be centered.

Male energy: Is focused, disciplined, objective, goal oriented, outward manifesting. It grants us a sense of individuality.

An excessive amount of male energy can lead to an outpouring of aggression and self-centeredness. Too much feminine energy can be controlling and possessive. I have 28 male energies and 18 female energies. I have more female energy than male energy. I need a 3 to 1 ratio of male energy to feminine energy. With 18 female energies, I would need 54 male energies to be balanced. It was explained to me that it is okay that I have more feminine energy than male energy as we live in male dominated society. It's important to be mindful of the imbalances that are associated with feminine energy as stated above.

Chapter 14

Conclusion

In conclusion, our emotions and psychological conditions are directly articulated within our energetic body. Discovering the emotions held by persons, in counseling, whether they be Sentient, Conscious or an Ascended Master, we look to release the individual of a disputatious emotional setting through active listening and enthusiastically recognizing and working to efficiently address the negative energy body that embraces and preserves emotions that no longer oblige the individual. There is only a small percentage of the human population that has discovered how our energy and emotional health play a vital role in our true happiness and living in our purpose. Healing can take place through psycho-energetic counseling and consistent meditation.

Your voice is the music of what you mean in the world; your uniqueness is your strength. One day, we will forget the indignant, the reason we wept and who caused us pain. We will finally comprehend that the secret of being free is not vengeance, but letting things reveal in their own way and own time. After all, what matters is not the first, but the last chapter of our life which shows how well we ran the race. So, smile, laugh, forgive, believe, and love all over again. When your soul speaks to you, listen.

Figure Index

References

Hay, L. (1999). *You Can Heal Your Life*. India. Hay House Publishers India.

Morgan, C. (2015, July 15). *360 Questions to Ask a Nuwaubian*.

Neteru, A. (2013). *Q2*. Houston, TX. Self-Published.

Neteru, A. (2016). *Flight of the Narcissist*. Houston, TX. Self-Published.

Orloff, J. (2004). *Positive Energy*. New York, NY. Harmony Books.

Orloff, J. (2009). *Emotional Freedom: Liberate Yourself From Negative Emotions and Transform*
   Your Life. New York, NY. Three Rivers Press.

Quill, S. (2007, August 8). *Antioch Missionary Baptist Church: This Old Church*. Retrieved from

   http://www.waymarking.com/waymarks/WM1ZDT_An
   tioch_Missionary_Baptist_Church_Houston_Texas

Rosario, F. (2017, March). *Pyloric Stenosis*. Retrieved from
   http://kidshealth.org/en/parents/pyloric-stenosis.html

Simpson, L. (2013). *The Book of Chakra Healing*. New York, NY. Sterling Publishing.

Some', M. (1994). *The Healing Wisdom of Africa*. Retrieved from
   http://www.englishwordplay.com/healingwisdom.html

Werner, J. (2016, September 10). Breaking Down Barriers. *Waco Tribune*, pp. 1C, 2C.

York-Westbrook, R. (2010.) *The Quantum Theory of Self-Empowerment*. Houston, TX.

Author's Page

Kirsten Westbrook, spiritually known as Maát Neftali, is a native Houstonian. She is an educator, dancer, author, poet, singer and actress. Her love for the arts goes back more than thirty years. A graduate of Barbizon Modeling School in 1994, Kirsten currently does plays with New Thought Theater, highlighting her martial arts skills through Wuji Sacred Arts. She played the role of General Asata in both "Rise of Mutapa" and "Rise of Mutapa II: Birth of the Goddesses." She dances weekly for The Center of Bio-Vibrational Science. Outside of the arts, Kirsten has a bachelor's degree in Finance from Texas A&M University, a Masters in Psycho Energetic Counseling from Southwest University of Sacred Studies, and another Master's in Education Administration from Lamar University. Before becoming an educator in 2006, Kirsten was a writer, editor and publisher of her own newspaper. Kirsten has been the talk show host for two shows. She has used her gifts of writing and speech to help others, starting at home with her three children.

www.ingramcontent.com/pod-product-compliance
Lightning Source LLC
Chambersburg PA
CBHW051828090426
42736CB00011B/1706